THE
POETRY OF NATURE

"As a fond Mother when the day is o'er."

THE POETRY OF NATURE: SELECTED BY HENRY VAN DYKE WITH MANY PHOTOGRAPHS FROM NATURE 🍃 🍃 🍃 🍃 🍃

Fredonia Books
Amsterdam, The Netherlands

The Poetry of Nature

Selected by
Henry van Dyke

ISBN: 1-4101-0762-0

Copyright © 2004 by Fredonia Books

Reprinted from the 1914 edition

Fredonia Books
Amsterdam, The Netherlands
http://www.fredoniabooks.com

All rights reserved, including the right to reproduce this book, or portions thereof, in any form.

In order to make original editions of historical works available to scholars at an economical price, this facsimile of the original edition of 1914 is reproduced from the best available copy and has been digitally enhanced to improve legibility, but the text remains unaltered to retain historical authenticity.

PREFACE

THE sixty Nature poems which I have chosen are full of various music. They utter the changing thoughts and feelings which are awakened in the heart of man by the procession of the seasons, the alternations of day and night, the balancing of the clouds and the journeying of the winds, the vision of the sea and the stars, the silent blossoming and fading of the flowers, the fleeting masonry of the snow, the flight and the return of our little brothers of the air. In all this wondrous pageant that passes before us we dimly perceive a meaning that corresponds to something within us. There are moments when this meaning seems to come nearer, to flash itself out more clearly, almost to lift the veil of beautiful form under which it moves. These clearer glimpses are the inspiration of the true poems of Nature. It is as if the great Mother herself were waking to consciousness in her human children, and speaking through their lips a part at least of that eternal thought and feeling which is transiently embodied in her visible forms.

Do not the best of these poems always bring to us, as we read them, at once a sense of familiarity and a sense of surprise? They tell us something

PREFACE

that belongs to us; their message comes from a world of which we ourselves are part; and it seems as if we must have always known it. But the telling of it so clearly is a sudden gleam of light falling into a place dim with shadows, and the newness of the vision fills us with an exquisite pleasure.

Some of the verses are but little lyrics, brief and delicate wafts of song, like Herrick's "Daffodils"; others are deeper and stronger, moving with a long-drawn, solemn music of thought, like Wordsworth's "Tintern Abbey," or sweeping us away with tempest-tones, like Shelley's "West Wind." But two things I have sought and found in all of them, simple or profound. They are true to the facts of Nature, faithful in observation of her works and ways; not daring to report falsely or foolishly of birds and flowers, of trees and rivers, but seeing with a lover's eyes, and painting with a lover's hand, loyal to the form as well as to the spirit. They are also clear and lucid in their utterance of the idea or emotion which is their life; not shapeless and incoherent, darkening the face of Nature by words without knowledge; but illuminating it with the light that comes from a spirit that can both think and feel.

There are many other Nature poems besides these

PREFACE

which are here gathered—some, indeed, of the most beautiful have been written by living poets. But these that follow are sixty of the best songs and sonnets, odes and reflective verses, written by poets who have finished their work and passed into new regions. Yet, as Keats said, they have also souls on earth, and they

teach us every day
Wisdom, though fled far away,

helping to make the world more beautiful and significant to those who are willing to live with Nature and learn of her.

HENRY VAN DYKE

CONTENTS

	PAGE
THE TITMOUSE. *By* RALPH WALDO EMERSON	1
THE OAK. *By* LORD TENNYSON	5
THE WHAUPS. *By* ROBERT LOUIS STEVENSON	5
FROST AT MIDNIGHT. *By* SAMUEL TAYLOR COLERIDGE	9
NIGHT. *By* JOSEPH BLANCO WHITE	12
UNDER THE GREENWOOD TREE. *As you like it*, II. v.	13
FAIRY LAND. *Midsummer Night's Dream*, II. i.	13
WHEN DAISIES PIED. *Love's Labour's Lost*, v. ii.	14
WHEN ICICLES HANG BY THE WALL. *Love's Labour's Lost*, v. ii.	15
THE FAIRY LIFE. *The Tempest*, v. i., I. ii.	16
EARLY SPRING. *By* LORD TENNYSON	17
TO A MOUNTAIN DAISY. *By* ROBERT BURNS	19
WALDEINSAMKEIT. *By* RALPH WALDO EMERSON	23
MY HEART LEAPS UP WHEN I BEHOLD. *By* WILLIAM WORDSWORTH	30
THE SANDPIPER. *By* CELIA THAXTER	30
DAFFODILS. *By* WILLIAM WORDSWORTH	33
HOME-THOUGHTS FROM ABROAD. *By* ROBERT BROWNING	35
TO DAFFODILS. *By* ROBERT HERRICK	36
THE THROSTLE. *By* LORD TENNYSON	37
TO THE CUCKOO. *By* JOHN LOGAN	41

CONTENTS

	PAGE
TO A SKYLARK. *By* Percy Bysshe Shelley	42
CORINNA'S GOING A-MAYING. *By* Robert Herrick	47
LINES WRITTEN IN EARLY SPRING. *By* William Wordsworth	49
ODE TO A NIGHTINGALE. *By* John Keats	51
TO A WATERFOWL. *By* William Cullen Bryant	54
THE RHODORA. *By* Ralph Waldo Emerson	55
THE GARDEN. *By* Andrew Marvell	56
TO THE DANDELION. *By* James Russell Lowell	59
SONG OF THE BROOK. *By* Lord Tennyson	61
TO A SKYLARK. *By* William Wordsworth	64
THE MOCKING BIRD. *By* Walt Whitman	65
SONGS FROM "PIPPA PASSES." *By* Robert Browning	71
SUMMER DAWN. *By* William Morris	71
TO THE HUMBLE-BEE. *By* Ralph Waldo Emerson	72
THE BAREFOOT BOY. *By* John Greenleaf Whittier	78
THE EVENING WIND. *By* William Cullen Bryant	83
THE MIDGES DANCE ABOON THE BURN. *By* Robert Tannahill	86

CONTENTS

	PAGE
BRIGHT STAR! WOULD I WERE STEADFAST AS THOU ART. *By* JOHN KEATS	87
DAYBREAK. *By* HENRY WADSWORTH LONGFELLOW	88
THE MARSHES OF GLYNN. *By* SIDNEY LANIER	89
THE CHAMBERED NAUTILUS. *By* OLIVER WENDELL HOLMES	95
EACH AND ALL. *By* RALPH WALDO EMERSON	96
IT IS A BEAUTEOUS EVENING, CALM AND FREE. *By* WILLIAM WORDSWORTH	98
THE WORLD IS TOO MUCH WITH US. *By* WILLIAM WORDSWORTH	99
TINTERN ABBEY. *By* WILLIAM WORDSWORTH	100
ODE TO EVENING *By* WILLIAM COLLINS	107
TEARS, IDLE TEARS. *By* LORD TENNYSON	111
THE LIGHT OF STARS. *By* HENRY WADSWORTH LONGFELLOW	112
TO AUTUMN. *By* JOHN KEATS	113
SONG. *By* LORD TENNYSON	115
TO A MOUSE. ROBERT BURNS	117
TO THE FRINGED GENTIAN. *By* WILLIAM CULLEN BRYANT	119
SEAWEED. *By* HENRY WADSWORTH LONGFELLOW	120
AUTUMN. *By* THOMAS HOOD	122
THE DEATH OF THE FLOWERS. *By* WILLIAM CULLEN BRYANT	125

CONTENTS

	PAGE
ODE TO THE WEST WIND. *By* PERCY BYSSHE SHELLEY	130
NATURE. *By* HENRY WADSWORTH LONGFELLOW	133
THE FIRST SNOWFALL. *By* JAMES RUSSELL LOWELL	134
INFLUENCE OF NATURAL OBJECTS. *By* WILLIAM WORDSWORTH	139
THE SNOWSTORM. *By* RALPH WALDO EMERSON	141
SONNET. *By* WILLIAM SHAKESPEARE	142
BLOW, BLOW, THOU WINTER WIND. *By* WILLIAM SHAKESPEARE	143
ON THE GRASSHOPPER AND CRICKET. *By* JOHN KEATS	144
THE DEATH OF THE OLD YEAR. *By* LORD TENNYSON	145

ILLUSTRATIONS

As a fond mother when the day is o'er	*Frontispiece*
All his leaves Fallen at length	*Page* 7
Under the greenwood tree	*To face p.* 14
Waldeinsamkeit	*Page* 23
Down in yon watery nook, Where bearded mists divide	,, 27
Daffodils	,, 33
Fair Daffodils	,, 39
The budding twigs spread out their fan	*To face p.* 50
Through verdurous glooms and winding mossy ways	,, 52
For men may come and men may go, But I go on for ever	,, 62
A privacy of glorious light is thine	, 64
Long days, and solid banks of flowers	*Page* 75
The Evening Wind	,, 83
A wind came up out of the sea, And said, " O mists, make room for me!"	*To face p.* 88
Glooms of the live-oaks, beautiful-braided and woven	,, 92
Ode to Evening	*Page* 107

ILLUSTRATIONS

Ah, sad and strange as in dark summer dawns	*To face p.* 112
Song	*Page* 115
Laden with seaweed from the rocks	*To face p.* 120
I saw old Autumn in the misty morn	,, 122
Heaped in the hollows of the grove, the autumn leaves lie dead	*Page* 127
Heaping field and highway With silence deep and white	,, 137
Blow, blow, thou winter wind	*To face p.* 144
The Death of the Old Year	*Page* 145

THE TITMOUSE

You shall not be overbold
When you deal with arctic cold,
As late I found my lukewarm blood
Chilled wading in the snow-choked wood.
How should I fight? my foeman fine
Has million arms to one of mine:
East, west, for aid I looked in vain,
East, west, north, south, are his domain.
Miles off, three dangerous miles, is home;
Must borrow his winds who there would come.
Up and away for life! be fleet!—
The frost-king ties my fumbling feet,
Sings in my ears, my hands are stones,
Curdles the blood to the marble bones,
Tugs at the heart-strings, numbs the sense,
And hems in life with narrowing fence.
Well, in this broad bed lie and sleep,—
The punctual stars will vigil keep,—
Embalmed by purifying cold;
The winds shall sing their dead-march old,
The snow is no ignoble shroud,
The moon thy mourner, and the cloud.

Softly,—but this way fate was pointing,
'Twas coming fast to such anointing,
When piped a tiny voice hard by,
Gay and polite, a cheerful cry,

THE POETRY OF NATURE

Chic-chicadeedee! saucy note
Out of sound heart and merry throat,
As if it said, "Good-day, good sir!
Fine afternoon, old passenger!
Happy to meet you in these places,
Where January brings new faces."

This poet, though he live apart,
Moved by his hospitable heart,
Sped, when I passed his sylvan fort,
To do the honours of his court,
As fits a feathered lord of land;
Flew near, with soft wing grazed my hand,
Hopped on the bough, then, darting low,
Prints his small impress in the snow,
Shows feats of his gymnastic play,
Head downward, clinging to the spray.

Here was this atom in full breath,
Hurling defiance at vast death;
This scrap of valour just for play
Fronts the north-wind in waistcoat grey,
As if to shame my weak behaviour;
I greeted loud my little saviour,
"You pet! What dost here? and what for?
In these woods, thy small Labrador,
At this pinch, wee San Salvador!
What fire burns in that little chest
So frolic, stout, and self-possest?

"Henceforth I wear no stripe but thine;
Ashes and jet all hues outshine.
Why are not diamonds black and grey,
To ape thy dare-devil array?
And I affirm, the spacious North
Exists to draw thy virtue forth.
I think no virtue goes with size;
The reason of all cowardice
Is, that men are overgrown,
And, to be valiant, must come down
To the titmouse dimension."

'Tis good-will makes intelligence,
And I began to catch the sense
Of my bird's song: "Live out of doors
In the great woods, on prairie floors.
I dine in the sun; when he sinks in the sea,
I too have a hole in a hollow tree;
And I like less when Summer beats
With stifling beams on these retreats,
Than noontide twilights which snow makes
With tempest of blinding flakes.
For well the soul, if stout within,
Can arm impregnably the skin;
And polar frost my frame defied,
Made of the air that blows outside."

With glad remembrance of my debt,
I homeward turn; farewell, my pet.

THE POETRY OF NATURE

When here again thy pilgrim comes,
He shall bring store of seeds and crumbs.
Doubt not, so long as earth has bread,
Thou first and foremost shalt be fed;
The Providence that is most large
Takes hearts like thine in special charge,
Helps who for their own need are strong,
And the sky doats on cheerful song.
Henceforth I prize thy wiry chant
O'er all that mass and minster vaunt;
For men mis-hear thy call in Spring,
As 't would accost some frivolous wing,
Crying out of the hazel copse, *Phe-be!*
And, in Winter, *Chic-a-dee-dee!*
I think old Cæsar must have heard
In northern Gaul my dauntless bird,
And, echoed in some frosty wold,
Borrowed thy battle-numbers bold.
And I will I write our annals new,
And thank thee for a better clew;
I, who dreamed not when I came here
To find the antidote of fear,
Now hear thee say in Roman key,
Pæan! Veni, vidi, vici.

RALPH WALDO EMERSON

THE OAK

Live thy Life,
   Young and old,
Like yon oak,
Bright in spring,
   Living gold;

Summer-rich
   Then; and then
Autumn-changed,
Soberer-hued
   Gold again.

All his leaves
   Fallen at length,
Look, he stands,
Trunk and bough,
   Naked strength.

Lord Tennyson

"THE WHAUPS"

Blows the wind to-day, and the sun and the rain are flying—
   Blows the wind on the moors to-day and now,
Where about the graves of martyrs the whaups are crying,
   My heart remembers how!

ALL HIS LEAVES
   FALLEN AT LENGTH
LOOK, HE STANDS,
TRUNK AND BOUGH,
   NAKED STRENGTH.

Grey, recumbent tombs of the dead in desert places,
  Standing stones on the vacant, red-wine moor,
Hills of sheep, and the homes of the silent vanished races,
  And winds, austere and pure!

Be it granted me to behold you again in dying,
  Hills of home! and I hear again the call—
Hear about the graves of the martyrs the pee-wees crying,
  And hear no more at all.

Robert Louis Stevenson

FROST AT MIDNIGHT

The Frost performs its secret ministry,
Unhelped by any wind. The owlet's cry
Came loud—and hark, again! loud as before.
The inmates of my cottage, all at rest,
Have left me to that solitude, which suits
Abstruser musings: save that at my side
My cradled infant slumbers peacefully.
'Tis calm indeed! so calm, that it disturbs
And vexes meditation with its strange
And extreme silentness. Sea, hill, and wood,
This populous village! Sea, and hill, and wood,
With all the numberless goings-on of life,

THE POETRY OF NATURE

Inaudible as dreams! the thin blue flame
Lies on my low-burnt fire, and quivers not;
Only that film, which fluttered on the grate,
Still flutters there, the sole unquiet thing.
Methinks, its motion in this hush of nature
Gives it dim sympathies with me who live,
Making it a companionable form,
Whose puny flaps and freaks the idling Spirit
By its own moods interprets, everywhere
Echo or mirror seeking of itself,
And makes a toy of Thought.

                                But O! how oft,
How oft, at school, with most believing mind,
Presageful, have I gazed upon the bars,
To watch that fluttering *stranger!* and as oft
With unclosed lids, already had I dreamt
Of my sweet birth-place, and the old church-tower,
Whose bells, the poor man's only music, rang
From morn to evening, all the hot Fairday,
So sweetly, that they stirred and haunted me
With a wild pleasure, falling on mine ear
Most like articulate sounds of things to come!
So gazed I, till the soothing things, I dreamt,
Lulled me to sleep, and sleep prolonged my dreams!
And so I brooded all the following morn,
Awed by the stern preceptor's face, mine eye
Fixed with mock study on my swimming book:
Save if the door half opened, and I snatched

A hasty glance, and still my heart leaped up,
For still I hoped to see the *stranger's* face,
Townsman, or aunt, or sister more beloved,
My play-mate when we both were clothed alike!

    Dear Babe, that sleepest cradled by my side,
Whose gentle breathings, heard in this deep calm,
Fill up the interspersèd vacancies
And momentary pauses of the thought!
My babe so beautiful! it thrills my heart
With tender gladness, thus to look at thee,
And think that thou shalt learn far other lore,
And in far other scenes! For I was reared
In the great city, pent 'mid cloisters dim,
And saw nought lovely but the sky and stars.
But *thou*, my babe! shalt wander like a breeze
By lakes and sandy shores, beneath the crags
Of ancient mountain, and beneath the clouds,
Which image in their bulk both lakes and shores
And mountain crags: so shalt thou see and hear
The lovely shapes and sounds intelligible
Of that eternal language, which thy God
Utters, who from eternity doth teach
Himself in all, and all things in himself.
Great universal Teacher! he shall mould
Thy spirit, and by giving make it ask.

    Therefore all seasons shall be sweet to thee,
Whether the summer clothe the general earth
With greenness, or the redbreast sit and sing

Betwixt the tufts of snow on the bare branch
Of mossy apple-tree, while the nigh thatch
Smokes in the sun-thaw; whether the eave-drops fall
Heard only in the trances of the blast,
Or if the secret ministry of the frost
Shall hang them up in silent icicles,
Quietly shining to the quiet Moon.
SAMUEL TAYLOR COLERIDGE

NIGHT

MYSTERIOUS Night! when our first parent knew
    Thee from report divine, and heard thy name,
    Did he not tremble for this goodly frame,
This glorious canopy of light and blue?
But through a curtain of translucent dew,
    Bathed in the rays of the great setting flame,
    Hesperus with the host of heaven came:
And lo! Creation broadened to man's view!

Who could have guessed such darkness lay concealed
    Within thy beams, O Sun? or who divined,
When bud and flower and insect lay revealed,
    Thou to such countless worlds had'st made us blind?
Why should we then shun Death with anxious strife?
    If Light conceals so much, wherefore not life?
JOSEPH BLANCO WHITE

UNDER THE GREENWOOD TREE

Under the greenwood tree
  Who loves to lie with me,
And turn his merry note
  Unto the sweet bird's throat—
Come hither, come hither, come hither!
  Here shall we see
    No enemy
But winter and rough weather.

Who doth ambition shun
  And loves to live i' the sun,
Seeking the food he eats
  And pleas'd with what he gets—
Come hither, come hither, come hither!
  Here shall he see
    No enemy
But winter and rough weather.

As You Like It, II. v

FAIRY LAND

Over hill, over dale,
  Thorough bush, thorough brier,
Over park, over pale,
  Thorough flood, thorough fire,

I do wander everywhere,
　Swifter than the moon's sphere;
And I serve the fairy queen,
　To dew her orbs upon the green;
The cowslips tall her pensioners be;
In their gold coats spots you see;
Those be rubies, fairy favours,
In those freckles live their savours;
I must go seek some dew-drops here,
And hang a pearl in every cowslip's ear.
　　　　Midsummer Night's Dream, II. i

WHEN DAISIES PIED

When daisies pied, and violets blue,
And lady-smocks all silver white,
And cuckoo-buds of yellow hue
Do paint the meadows with delight,
The cuckoo then, on every tree,
Mocks married men; for thus sings he,
　Cuckoo!
Cuckoo, Cuckoo! O word of fear,
Unpleasing to a married ear!

When shepherds piped on oaten straws,
And merry larks are ploughmen's clocks,
When turtles tread, and rooks and daws,
And maidens bleach their summer smocks,
The cuckoo then, on every tree,

"Under the Greenwood Tree"

>   Mocks married men; for thus sings he,
>   Cuckoo!
>   Cuckoo, Cuckoo!   O word of fear,
>   Unpleasing to a married ear.
>
>   <div align="right"><i>Love's Labour's Lost</i>, v. ii</div>

WHEN ICICLES HANG BY THE WALL

>   When icicles hang by the wall,
>   And Dick the shepherd blows his nail,
>   And Tom bears logs into the hall,
>   And milk comes frozen home in pail,
>   When blood is nipp'd, and ways be foul,
>   Then nightly sings the staring owl,
>   To-whit!
>   To-who!—a merry note,
>   While greasy Joan doth keel the pot.
>
>   When all aloud the wind doth blow,
>   And coughing drowns the parson's saw,
>   And birds sit brooding in the snow,
>   And Marian's nose looks red and raw,
>   When roasted crabs hiss in the bowl,
>   Then nightly sings the staring owl,
>   To-whit!
>   To-who!—a merry note,
>   While greasy Joan doth keel the pot.
>
>   <div align="right"><i>Love's Labour's Lost</i>, v. ii</div>

THE FAIRY LIFE

I

Where the bee sucks, there suck I;
In a cowslip's bell I lie;
There I couch, when owls do cry:
On the bat's back I do fly
  After summer merrily.
Merrily, merrily, shall I live now,
Under the blossom that hangs on the bough!

The Tempest, v. i

II

Come unto these yellow sands,
And then take hands:
Courtsied when you have and kiss'd
The wild waves whist,
Foot it featly here and there;
And sweet sprites, the burthen bear.
  Hark, hark!
    Bow-wow.
  The watch-dogs bark:
    Bow-wow.
  Hark, hark! I hear
The strain of strutting chanticleer
  Cry, Cock-a-diddle-dow!

The Tempest, i. ii.

EARLY SPRING

Once more the Heavenly Power
    Makes all things new,
And domes the red-plow'd hills
    With loving blue;
The blackbirds have their wills,
    The throstles too.

Opens a door in Heaven;
    From skies of glass
A Jacob's ladder falls
    On greening grass,
And o'er the mountain walls
    Young angels pass.

Before them fleets the shower,
    And burst the buds,
And shine the level lands,
    And flash the floods;
The stars are from their hands
    Flung thro' the woods.

The woods with living airs
    How softly fann'd,
Light airs from where the deep,
    All down the sand,
Is breathing in his sleep,
    Heard by the land.

O follow, leaping blood,
　　The season's lure!
O heart, look down and up
　　Serene, secure,
Warm as the crocus cup,
　　Like snowdrops, pure!

Past, Future glimpse and fade
　　Thro' some slight spell,
A gleam from yonder vale,
　　Some far blue fell,
And sympathies, how frail,
　　In sound and smell!

Till at thy chuckled note,
　　Thou twinkling bird,
The fairy fancies range,
　　And, lightly stirr'd,
Ring little bells of change
　　From word to word.

For now the Heavenly Power
　　Makes all things new,
And thaws the cold, and fills
　　The flower with dew;
The blackbirds have their wills,
　　The poets too.

　　　　　　　　LORD TENNYSON

TO A MOUNTAIN DAISY

ON TURNING ONE DOWN WITH THE PLOUGH IN APRIL, 1786

Wee, modest, crimson-tippèd flower,
Thou 's met me in an evil hour;
For I maun crush amang the stoure
    Thy slender stem;
To spare thee now is past my power,
    Thou bonnie gem.

Alas! it's no thy neebor sweet,
The bonnie lark, companion meet,
Bending thee 'mang the dewy weet,
    Wi' spreckled breast!
When upward-springing, blithe, to greet
    The purpling east.

Cauld blew the bitter-biting north
Upon thy early, humble birth;
Yet cheerfully thou glinted forth
    Amid the storm,
Scarce reared above the parent-earth
    Thy tender form.

The flaunting flowers our gardens yield,
High sheltering woods and wa's maun
    shield;
But thou, beneath the random bield
    O' clod or stane,
Adorns the histie stibble-field,
    Unseen, alane.

There, in thy scanty mantle clad,
Thy snawie bosom sun-ward spread,
Thou lifts thy unassuming head
    In humble guise;
But now the share uptears thy bed,
    And low thou lies!

Such is the fate of artless maid,
Sweet floweret of the rural shade!
By love's simplicity betrayed,
    And guileless trust;
Till she, like thee, all soiled, is laid
    Low i' the dust.

Such is the fate of simple Bard,
On Life's rough ocean luckless starred
Unskilful he to note the card
    Of prudent lore,
Till billows rage, and gales blow hard,
    And whelm him o'er!

Such fate to suffering Worth is given,
Who long with wants and woes has striven,
By human pride or cunning driven
    To misery's brink;
Till, wrenched of every stay but Heaven,
    He, ruined, sink!

Even thou who mourn'st the Daisy's fate,
That fate is thine—no distant date;
Stern Ruin's ploughshare drives elate,
    Full on thy bloom,
Till crushed beneath the furrow's weight
    Shall be thy doom!

ROBERT BURNS

WALDEINSAMKEIT

I do not count the hours I spend
In wandering by the sea;
The forest is my loyal friend,
Like God it useth me.

In plains that room for shadows make
Of skirting hills to lie,
Bound in by streams which give and take
Their colours from the sky;

Or on the mountain-crest sublime,
Or down the oaken glade,
O what have I to do with time?
For this the day was made.

Cities of mortals woebegone
Fantastic care derides,
But in the serious landscape lone
Stern benefit abides.

Sheen will tarnish, honey cloy,
And merry is only a mask of sad,
But, sober on a fund of joy,
The woods at heart are glad.

There the great Planter plants
Of fruitful worlds the grain,
And with a million spells enchants
The souls that walk in pain.

Still on the seeds of all he made
The rose of beauty burns;
Through times that wear and forms that fade,
Immortal youth returns.

The black ducks mounting from the lake,
The pigeon in the pines,
The bittern's boom, a desert make
Which no false art refines.

Down in yon watery nook,
Where bearded mists divide

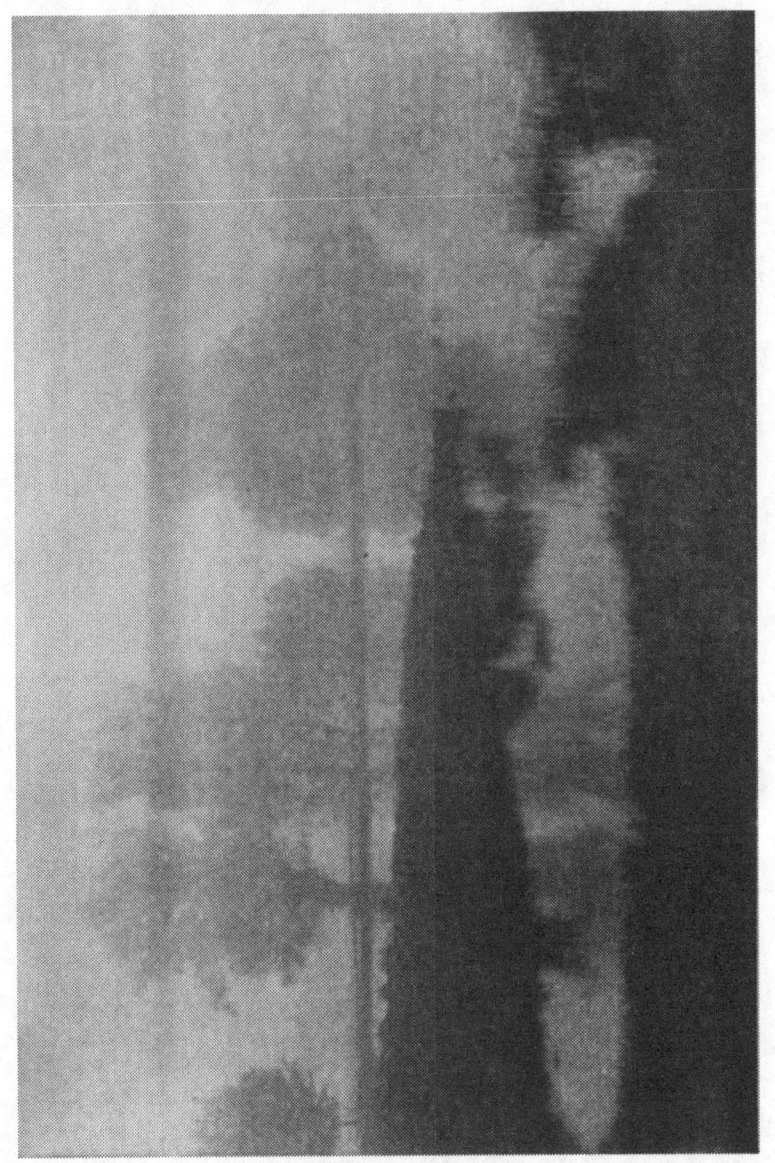

THE POETRY OF NATURE

Down in yon watery nook,
Where bearded mists divide,
The grey old gods whom Chaos knew
The sires of Nature, hide.

Aloft, in secret veins of air,
Blows the sweet breath of song,
O, few to scale those uplands dare,
Though they to all belong!

See thou bring not to field or stone
The fancies found in books;
Leave author's eyes, and fetch your own,
To brave the landscape's looks.

Oblivion, here thy wisdom is,
Thy thrift, the sleep of cares;
For a proud idleness like this
Crowns all thy mean affairs.

RALPH WALDO EMERSON

"MY HEART LEAPS UP WHEN I BEHOLD"

My heart leaps up when I behold
    A rainbow in the sky:
So was it when my life began;
So is it now I am a man;
So be it when I shall grow old,
    Or let me die!
The Child is father of the Man;
And I could wish my days to be
Bound each to each by natural piety.
WILLIAM WORDSWORTH

THE SANDPIPER

Across the narrow beach we flit,
    One little sandpiper and I;
And fast I gather, bit by bit,
    The scattered driftwood bleached and dry.
The wild waves reach their hands for it,
    The wild wind raves, the tide runs high,
As up and down the beach we flit—
    One little sandpiper and I.

Above our heads the sullen clouds
    Scud black and swift across the sky:
Like silent ghosts in misty shrouds
    Stand out the white lighthouses high.

Almost as far as eye can reach
　　I see the close-reefed vessels fly.
As fast we flit along the beach—
　　One little sandpiper and I.

I watch him as he skims along,
　　Uttering his sweet and mournful cry.
He starts not at my fitful song,
　　Or flash of fluttering drapery;
He has no thought of any wrong;
　　He scans me with a fearless eye:
Staunch friends are we, well tried and strong,
　　The little sandpiper and I.

Comrade, where wilt thou be to-night
　　When the loosed storm breaks furiously?
My driftwood fire will burn so bright!
　　To what warm shelter canst thou fly?
I do not fear for thee, though wroth
　　The tempest rushes through the sky:
For are we not God's children both,
　　Thou, little sandpiper, and I?

CELIA THAXTER

DAFFODILS

I WANDER'D lonely as a cloud
   That floats on high o'er vales and hills,
When all at once I saw a crowd,
   A host, of golden daffodils;
Beside the lake, beneath the trees,
Fluttering and dancing in the breeze.

    Continuous as the stars that shine
        And twinkle on the Milky Way,
They stretch'd in never ending line
    Along the margin of a bay:
Ten thousand saw I at a glance,
    Tossing their heads in sprightly dance.

The waves beside them danced; but they
    Outdid the sparkling waves in glee:
A poet could not but be gay,
    In such a jocund company:
I gazed—and gazed—but little thought
What wealth the show to me had brought:

For oft, when on my couch I lie
    In vacant or in pensive mood,
They flash upon that inward eye
    Which is the bliss of solitude;
And then my heart with pleasure fills,
And dances with the daffodils.
                      WILLIAM WORDSWORTH

HOME-THOUGHTS FROM ABROAD

Oh, to be in England
    Now that April's there,
And whoever wakes in England
    Sees, some morning, unaware,
That the lowest boughs and the brushwood sheaf
Round the elm-tree bole are in tiny leaf,

While the chaffinch sings on the orchard bough
In England—now!

And after April, when May follows,
And the whitethroat builds, and all the swallows!
Hark, where my blossomed pear-tree in the hedge
  Leans to the field and scatters on the clover
Blossoms and dewdrops—at the bent spray's edge—
  That's the wise thrush; he sings each song twice over,
Lest you should think he never could recapture
The first fine careless rapture!
And though the fields look rough with hoary dew,
All will be gay when noontide wakes anew
The buttercups, the little children's dower
—Far brighter than this gaudy melon-flower!

ROBERT BROWNING

TO DAFFODILS

Fair Daffodils, we weep to see
  You haste away so soon:
As yet the early-rising Sun
  Has not attain'd his noon.
    Stay, stay,
  Until the hasting day
    Has run
  But to the even-song;
And, having pray'd together, we
  Will go with you along.

We have short time to stay, as you,
  We have as short a Spring;
As quick a growth to meet decay,
  As you, or any thing.
    We die,
  As your hours do, and dry
    Away,
  Like to the Summer's rain;
Or as the pearls of morning's dew,
  Ne'er to be found again.

ROBERT HERRICK

THE THROSTLE

"Summer is coming, summer is coming.
  I know it, I know it, I know it.
Light again, leaf again, life again, love again,"
  Yes, my wild little Poet.

Sing the new year in under the blue.
  Last year you sang it as gladly.
"New, new, new, new!" Is it then *so* new
  That you should carol so madly?

"Love again, song again, nest again, young again,"
  Never a prophet so crazy!
And hardly a daisy as yet, little friend,
  See, there is hardly a daisy.

Fair Daffodils

"Here again, here, here, here, happy year!"
  O warble unchidden, unbidden!
Summer is coming, is coming, my dear,
  And all the winters are hidden.
                              LORD TENNYSON

TO THE CUCKOO

HAIL, beauteous stranger of the grove!
  Thou messenger of spring!
Now Heaven repairs thy rural seat.
  And woods thy welcome sing.

What time the daisy decks the green,
  Thy certain voice we hear;
Hast thou a star to guide thy path,
  Or mark the rolling year?

Delightful visitant! with thee
  I hail the time of flowers,
And hear the sound of music sweet
  From birds among the bowers.

The schoolboy, wandering through the wood
  To pull the primrose gay,
Starts, the new voice of Spring to hear,
  And imitates thy lay.

What time the pea puts on the bloom,
  Thou fliest thy vocal vale,
An annual guest in other lands.
  Another spring to hail.

Sweet bird! thy bower is ever green,
  Thy sky is ever clear;
Thou hast no sorrow in thy song,
  No winter in thy year!

O, could I fly, I'd fly with thee!
  We'd make, with joyful wing,
Our annual visit o'er the globe,
  Companions of the Spring.

JOHN LOGAN

TO A SKYLARK

Hail to thee, blithe Spirit!
  Bird thou never wert,
That from heaven, or near it,
  Pourest thy full heart
In profuse strains of unpremeditated art.

Higher still and higher
  From the earth thou springest
Like a cloud of fire;
  The blue deep thou wingest,
And singing still dost soar, and soaring ever singest.

In the golden lightning
   Of the sunken sun,
O'er which clouds are brightening,
   Thou dost float and run;
Like an unbodied joy whose race is just begun.

The pale purple even
   Melts around thy flight;
Like a star of heaven
   In the broad daylight,
Thou art unseen, but yet I hear thy shrill delight.

Keen as are the arrows
   Of that silver sphere,
Whose intense lamp narrows
   In the white dawn clear,
Until we hardly see, we feel that it is there.

All the earth and air
   With thy voice is loud,
As, when night is bare,
   From one lonely cloud
The moon rains out her beams, and heaven is
   overflow'd.

What thou art we know not;
   What is most like thee?
From rainbow clouds there flow not
   Drops so bright to see,
As from thy presence showers a rain of melody.

Like a poet hidden
   In the light of thought,
Singing hymns unbidden,
   Till the world is wrought
To sympathy with hopes and fears it heeded not:

Like a high-born maiden
   In a palace-tower,
Soothing her love-laden
   Soul in secret hour
With music sweet as love, which overflows her bower:

Like a glow-worm golden
   In a dell of dew,
Scattering unbeholden
   Its aerial hue
Among the flowers and grass, which screen it from the view:

Like a rose embower'd
   In its own green leaves,
By warm winds deflower'd,
   Till the scent it gives
Makes faint with too much sweet these heavy-wingèd thieves.

Sound of vernal showers
   On the twinkling grass,
Rain-awaken'd flowers,
   All that ever was
Joyous, and clear, and fresh, thy music doth surpass:

Teach us, sprite or bird,
    What sweet thoughts are thine:
I have never heard
    Praise of love or wine
That panted forth a flood of rapture so divine.

Chorus Hymeneal,
    Or triumphal chaunt,
Match'd with thine would be all
    But an empty vaunt,
A thing wherein we feel there is some hidden want.

What objects are the fountains
    Of thy happy strain?
What fields, or waves, or mountains?
    What shapes of sky or plain?
What love of thy own kind? what ignorance of pain?

With thy clear keen joyance
    Languor cannot be:
Shadow of annoyance
    Never came near thee:
Thou lovest; but ne'er knew love's sad satiety.

Waking or asleep,
    Thou of death must deem
Things more true and deep
    Than we mortals dream,
Or how could thy notes flow in such a crystal stream?

THE POETRY OF NATURE

  We look before and after,
   And pine for what is not:
  Our sincerest laughter
   With some pain is fraught;
Our sweetest songs are those that tell of saddest thought.

  Yet if we could scorn
   Hate, and pride, and fear;
  If we were things born
   Not to shed a tear,
I know not how thy joy we ever should come near.

  Better than all measures
   Of delightful sound,
  Better than all treasures
   That in books are found,
Thy skill to poet were, thou scorner of the ground!

  Teach me half the gladness
   That thy brain must know,
  Such harmonious madness
   From my lips would flow,
The world should listen then, as I am listening now.
        PERCY BYSSHE SHELLEY

CORINNA'S GOING A-MAYING

Get up, get up for shame! The blooming morn
Upon her wings presents the god unshorn.
    See how Aurora throws her fair
    Fresh-quilted colours through the air:
    Get up, sweet slug-a-bed, and see
    The dew bespangling herb and tree!
Each flower has wept and bow'd toward the east
Above an hour since, yet you not drest;
    Nay! not so much as out of bed?
    When all the birds have matins said
    And sung their thankful hymns, 'tis sin,
    Nay, profanation, to keep in,
When as a thousand virgins on this day
Spring, sooner than the lark, to fetch in May.

Rise and put on your foliage, and be seen
To come forth, like the spring-time, fresh and green,
    And sweet as Flora. Take no care
    For jewels for your gown or hair:
    Fear not; the leaves will strew
    Gems in abundance upon you:
Besides, the childhood of the day has kept,
Against you come, some orient pearls unwept.
    Come, and receive them while the light
    Hangs on the dew-locks of the night:
    And Titan on the eastern hill
    Retires himself, or else stands still

Till you come forth! Wash, dress, be brief in praying:
Few beads are best when once we go a-Maying.

Come, my Corinna, come; and, coming, mark
How each field turns a street, each street a park,
    Made green and trimm'd with trees: see how
    Devotion gives each house a bough
    Or branch: each porch, each door, ere this,
    An ark, a tabernacle is,
Made up of white-thorn neatly interwove;
As if here were those cooler shades of love.
    Can such delights be in the street
    And open fields, and we not see't?
    Come, we'll abroad: and let's obey
    The proclamation made for May,
And sin no more, as we have done, by staying;
But, my Corinna, come, let's go a-Maying.

There's not a budding boy or girl this day
But is got up and gone to bring in May.
    A deal of youth ere this is come
    Back, and with white-thorn laden home.
    Some have despatch'd their cakes and cream,
    Before that we have left to dream:
And some have wept and woo'd, and plighted troth,
And chose their priest, ere we can cast off sloth:
    Many a green-gown has been given;
    Many a kiss, both odd and even:

> Many a glance, too, has been sent
> From out the eye, love's firmament;
> Many a jest told of the keys betraying
> This night, and locks pick'd: yet we're not a-Maying!
>
> Come, let us go, while we are in our prime;
> And take the harmless folly of the time.
> We shall grow old apace, and die
> Before we know our liberty.
> Our life is short, and our days run
> As fast away as does the sun;
> And, as a vapour or a drop of rain,
> Once lost, can ne'er be found again,
> So when or you or I are made
> A fable, song, or fleeting shade,
> All love, all liking, all delight
> Lies drown'd with us in endless night.
> Then while time serves, and we are but decaying,
> Come, my Corinna, come, let's go a-Maying.

ROBERT HERRICK

LINES WRITTEN IN EARLY SPRING

> I HEARD a thousand blended notes,
> While in a grove I sate reclined,
> In that sweet mood when pleasant thoughts
> Bring sad thoughts to the mind.

To her fair works did Nature link
  The human soul that through me ran;
And much it grieved my heart to think
  What man has made of man.

Through primrose tufts, in that green bower,
  The periwinkle trailed its wreaths;
And 'tis my faith that every flower
  Enjoys the air it breathes.

The birds around me hopped and played,
  Their thoughts I cannot measure:—
But the least motion which they made
  It seemed a thrill of pleasure.

The budding twigs spread out their fan,
  To catch the breezy air,
And I must think, do all I can,
  That there was pleasure there.

If this belief from heaven be sent,
  If such be Nature's holy plan,
Have I not reason to lament
  What man has made of man?

WILLIAM WORDSWORTH

"The budding twigs spread out their fan"

ODE TO A NIGHTINGALE

My heart aches, and a drowsy numbness pains
    My sense, as though of hemlock I had drunk,
Or emptied some dull opiate to the drains
    One minute past, and Lethe-wards had sunk:
'Tis not through envy of thy happy lot,
    But being too happy in thy happiness,—
        That thou, light-wingèd Dryad of the trees,
        In some melodious plot
Of beechen green, and shadows numberless,
    Singest of summer in full-throated ease.

O for a draught of vintage that hath been
    Cool'd a long age in the deep-delved earth,
Tasting of Flora and the country-green,
    Dance, and Provençal song, and sunburnt mirth!
O for a beaker full of the warm South,
    Full of the true, the blushful Hippocrene,
        With beaded bubbles winking at the brim,
        And purple-stainèd mouth;
That I might drink, and leave the world unseen,
    And with thee fade away into the forest dim:

Fade far away, dissolve, and quite forget
    What thou among the leaves hast never known,
The weariness, the fever, and the fret
    Here, where men sit and hear each other groan;

Where palsy shakes a few, sad, last grey hairs,
    Where youth grows pale, and spectre-thin, and dies;
        Where but to think is to be full of sorrow
        And leaden-eyed despairs,
    Where Beauty cannot keep her lustrous eyes,
        Or new Love pine at them beyond to-morrow.

Away! away! for I will fly to thee,
    Not charioted by Bacchus and his pards,
But on the viewless wings of Poesy,
    Though the dull brain perplexes and retards:
Already with thee! tender is the night,
    And haply the Queen-Moon is on her throne,
        Cluster'd around by all her starry Fays;
        But here there is no light,
    Save what from heaven is with the breezes blown
        Through verdurous glooms and winding mossy ways.

I cannot see what flowers are at my feet,
    Nor what soft incense hangs upon the boughs,
But in embalmèd darkness, guess each sweet
    Wherewith the seasonable month endows
The grass, the thicket, and the fruit-tree wild;
    White hawthorn, and the pastoral eglantine;
        Fast fading violets cover'd up in leaves;
        And mid-May's eldest child,
    The coming musk-rose, full of dewy wine,
        The murmurous haunt of flies on summer eves.

"Through verdurous glooms and winding mossy ways".

Darkling I listen; and, for many a time
   I have been half in love with easeful Death,
Call'd him soft names in many a musèd rhyme,
   To take into the air my quiet breath;
Now more than ever seems it rich to die,
   To cease upon the midnight with no pain,
     While thou art pouring forth thy soul abroad
       In such an ecstasy!
     Still wouldst thou sing, and I have ears in vain—
      To thy high requiem become a sod.

Thou wast not born for death, immortal Bird!
   No hungry generations tread thee down;
The voice I hear this passing night was heard
   In ancient days by emperor and clown:
Perhaps the self-same song that found a path
   Through the sad heart of Ruth, when, sick for home,
     She stood in tears amid the alien corn;
       The same that oft-times hath
     Charm'd magic casements, opening on the foam
      Of perilous seas, in faery lands forlorn.

Forlorn! the very word is like a bell
   To tell me back from thee to my sole self!
Adieu! the fancy cannot cheat so well
   As she is fam'd to do, deceiving elf.
Adieu! adieu! thy plaintive anthem fades
   Past the near meadows, over the still stream,

Up the hill-side; and now 'tis buried deep
  In the next valley-glades:
Was it a vision, or a waking dream?
  Fled is that music:—Do I wake or sleep?
                                          JOHN KEAT

TO A WATERFOWL

Whither, midst falling dew,
While glow the heavens with the last steps of day,
Far, through their rosy depths, dost thou pursue
  Thy solitary way?

Vainly the fowler's eye
Might mark thy distant flight to do thee wrong,
As, darkly painted on the crimson sky,
  Thy figure floats along.

Seek'st thou the plashy brink
Of weedy lake, or marge of river wide,
Or where the rocking billows rise and sink
  On the chafed ocean-side?

There is a Power whose care
Teaches thy way along that pathless coast—
The desert and illimitable air—
  Lone wandering, but not lost.

All day thy wings have fanned,
At that far height, the cold, thin atmosphere,
Yet stoop not, weary, to the welcome land,
    Though the dark night is near.

And soon that toil shall end;
Soon shalt thou find a summer home, and rest,
And scream among thy fellows; reeds shall bend,
    Soon, o'er thy sheltered nest.

Thou'rt gone, the abyss of heaven
Hath swallowed up thy form; yet, on my heart
Deeply hath sunk the lesson thou hast given,
    And shall not soon depart.

He who, from zone to zone,
Guides through the boundless sky thy certain flight,
In the long way that I must tread alone,
    Will lead my steps aright.
                      WILLIAM CULLEN BRYANT

THE RHODORA
ON BEING ASKED, WHENCE IS THE FLOWER?

IN May, when sea-winds pierced our solitudes,
I found the fresh Rhodora in the woods,
Spreading its leafless blooms in a damp nook,
To please the desert and the sluggish brook.

The purple petals, fallen in the pool,
Made the black water with their beauty gay;
Here might the red-bird come his plumes to cool,
And court the flower that cheapens his array.
Rhodora! if the sages ask thee why
This charm is wasted on the earth and sky,
Tell them, dear, that if eyes were made for seeing,
Then Beauty is its own excuse for being:
Why thou wert there, O rival of the rose!
I never thought to ask, I never knew:
But, in my simple ignorance, suppose
The self-same Power that brought me there brought
    you.

Ralph Waldo Emerson

THE GARDEN

How vainly men themselves amaze,
  To win the palm, the oak, or bays;
And their incessant labours see
  Crown'd from some single herb or tree,
Whose short and narrow-vergèd shade
  Does prudently their toils upbraid;
While all the flowers and trees do close,
  To weave the garlands of Repose.

Fair Quiet, have I found thee here,
  And Innocence thy sister dear?

Mistaken long, I sought you then
  In busy companies of men.
Your sacred plants, if here below,
  Only among plants will grow;
Society is all but rude
  To this delicious solitude.

No white nor red was ever seen
  So amorous as this lovely green.
Fond lovers, cruel as their flame,
  Cut in these trees their mistress' name:
Little, alas, they know or heed
  How far these beauties hers exceed!
Fair trees! where s'e'er your bark I wound,
  No name shall but your own be found.

When we have run our passion's heat,
  Love hither makes his best retreat.
The gods, that mortal beauty chase,
  Still in a tree did end their race;
Apollo hunted Daphne so
  Only that she might laurel grow;
And Pan did after Syrinx speed
  Not as a nymph, but for a reed.

What wondrous life is this I lead!
  Ripe apples drop about my head;
The luscious clusters of the vine
  Upon my mouth do crush their wine;

    The nectarine and curious peach
      Into my hands themselves do reach;
    Stumbling on melons, as I pass,
      Ensnared with flowers, I fall on grass.

    Meanwhile the mind from pleasure less
      Withdraws into its happiness;
    The mind, that ocean where each kind
      Does straight its own resemblance find;
    Yet it creates, transcending these,
      Far other worlds, and other seas,
    Annihilating all that's made
      To a green thought in a green shade.

    Here at the fountain's sliding foot,
      Or at some fruit tree's mossy root,
    Casting the body's vest aside,
      My soul into the boughs does glide;
    There, like a bird, it sits and sings,
      Then whets and combs its silver wings,
    And, till prepared for longer flight,
      Waves in its plumes the various light.

Such was that happy garden-state
    While man there walk'd without a mate:
After a place so pure and sweet,
    What other help could yet be meet!
But 'twas beyond a mortal's share
    To wander solitary there:
Two paradises 'twere in one,
    To live in paradise alone.

How well the skilful gardener drew
  Of flowers and herbs this dial new!
Where, from above, the milder sun
  Does through a fragrant zodiac run,
And, as it works, the industrious bee
  Computes its time as well as we.
How could such sweet and wholesome hours
  Be reckoned, but with herbs and flowers?

                          ANDREW MARVELL

TO THE DANDELION

DEAR common flower, that grow'st beside the way,
Fringing the dusty road with harmless gold,
  First pledge of blithesome May,
Which children pluck, and, full of pride uphold,
High-hearted buccaneers, o'erjoyed that they
An Eldorado in the grass have found,
  Which not the rich earth's ample round
May match in wealth, thou art more dear to me
Than all the prouder summer-blooms may be.

Gold such as thine ne'er drew the Spanish prow
Through the primeval hush of Indian seas,
  Nor wrinkled the lean brow
Of age, to rob the lover's heart of ease;
'Tis the Spring's largess, which she scatters now
To rich and poor alike, with lavish hand,

THE POETRY OF NATURE

    Though most hearts never understand
To take it at God's value, but pass by
The offered wealth with unrewarded eye.

Thou art my tropics and mine Italy;
To look at thee unlocks a warmer clime;
    The eyes thou givest me
Are in the heart, and heed not space or time:
Not in mid-June the golden-cuirassed bee
Feels a more summer-like warm ravishment
    In the white lily's breezy tent,
His fragrant Sybaris, than I, when first
From the dark green thy yellow circles burst.

Then think I of deep shadows in the grass,
Of meadows where in sun the cattle graze,
    Where, as the breezes pass,
The gleaming rushes lean a thousand ways,
Of leaves that slumber in a cloudy mass,
Or whiten in the wind, of waters blue
    That from the distance sparkle through
Some woodland gap, and of a sky above,
Where one white cloud like a stray lamb doth move.

My childhood's earliest thoughts are linked with thee;
The sight of thee calls back the robin's song,
    Who, from the dark old tree
Beside the door, sang clearly all day long,
And I, secure in childish piety,
Listened as if I heard an angel sing

      With news from Heaven, which he could bring
Fresh every day to my untainted ears
When birds and flowers and I were happy peers.

How like a prodigal doth Nature seem,
When thou, for all thy gold, so common art!
    Thou teachest me to deem
More sacredly of every human heart,
Since each reflects in joy its scanty gleam
Of Heaven, and could some wondrous secret show,
    Did we but pay the love we owe,
And with a child's undoubting wisdom look
On all these living pages of God's book.
JAMES RUSSELL LOWELL

SONG OF THE BROOK

  I COME from haunts of coot and hern,
    I make a sudden sally,
  And sparkle out among the fern,
    To bicker down a valley.

  By thirty hills I hurry down,
    Or slip between the ridges,
  By twenty thorps, a little town,
    And half a hundred bridges.

THE POETRY OF NATURE

    Till last by Philip's farm I flow
      To join the brimming river,
    For men may come and men may go,
      But I go on for ever.

    I chatter over stony ways,
      In little sharps and trebles,
    I bubble into eddying bays,
      I babble on the pebbles.

    With many a curve my banks I fret
      By many a field and fallow,
    And many a fairy foreland set
      With willow-weed and mallow.

    I chatter, chatter, as I flow
      To join the brimming river;
    For men may come and men may go,
      But I go on for ever.

    I wind about, and in and out,
      With here a blossom sailing,
    And here and there a lusty trout,
      And here and there a grayling,

    And here and there a foamy flake
      Upon me, as I travel
    With many a silvery waterbreak
      Above the golden gravel,

"For men may come and men may go, but I go on for ever".

      And draw them all along, and flow
        To join the brimming river;
    For men may come and men may go,
        But I go on for ever.

      I steal by lawns and grassy plots,
        I slide by hazel covers;
      I move the sweet forget-me-nots
        That grow for happy lovers.

      I slip, I slide, I gloom, I glance,
        Among my skimming swallows;
      I make the netted sunbeam dance
        Against my sandy shallows.

      I murmur under moon and stars
        In brambly wildernesses;
      I linger by my shingly bars;
        I loiter round my cresses;

      And out again I curve and flow
        To join the brimming river;
    For men may come and men may go,
        But I go on for ever.
LORD TENNYSON

TO A SKYLARK

Ethereal minstrel! pilgrim of the sky!
   Dost thou despise the earth where cares abound?
Or while the wings aspire, are heart and eye
   Both with thy nest upon the dewy ground?
Thy nest which thou canst drop into at will,
Those quivering wings composed, that music still!

[To the last point of vision, and beyond,
   Mount, daring warbler!—that love-prompted strain
—'Twixt thee and thine a never-failing bond—
   Thrills not the less the bosom of the plain:
Yet might'st thou seem, proud privilege! to sing
All independent of the leafy Spring.]

Leave to the nightingale her shady wood;
   A privacy of glorious light is thine;
Whence thou dost pour upon the world a flood
   Of harmony, with instinct more divine;
Type of the wise who soar, but never roam;
True to the kindred points of Heaven and Home.

WILLIAM WORDSWORTH

"A privacy of Glorious Light is thine."

THE MOCKING BIRD

(FROM "OUT OF THE CRADLE")

Once Paumanok,
When the lilac-scent was in the air, and the Fifth-
    month grass was growing,
Up this seashore in some briars,
Two feathered guests from Alabama, two together,
And their nest, and four light-green eggs spotted
    with brown.
And every day the he-bird to and fro near at hand,
And every day the she-bird crouched on her nest,
    silent, with bright eyes,
And every day I, a curious boy, never too close,
    never disturbing them,
Cautiously peering, absorbing, translating.

"Shine! shine! shine!
Pour down your warmth, great Sun!
While we bask, we two together.

"Two together!
Winds blow south, or winds blow north,
Day come white, or night come black,
Home, or rivers and mountains from home,
Singing all time, minding no time,
While we two keep together."

    Till of a sudden,
Maybe killed, unknown to her mate,
One forenoon the she-bird crouched not on the nest,
Nor returned that afternoon, nor the next,
Nor ever appeared again.

And thenceforward all summer in the sound of the sea,
And at night under the full of the moon in calmer
    weather,
Over the hoarse surging of the sea,
Or flitting from briar to briar by day,
I saw, I heard at intervals the remaining one, the
    he-bird,
The solitary guest from Alabama.

    "Blow! blow! blow!
Blow up sea-winds along Paumanok's shore;
I wait and I wait, till you blow my mate to me."

    Yes, when the stars glistened,
All night long on the prong of a moss-scalloped stake,
Down almost amid the slapping waves,
Sat the lone singer wonderful causing tears.

    He called on his mate,
He poured forth the meanings which I of all men
    know.
Yes, my brother, I know,—
The rest might not, but I have treasured every note,

For more than once dimly down to the beach
    gliding,
Silent, avoiding the moonbeams, blending myself
    with the shadows,
Recalling now the obscure shapes, the echoes, the
    sounds and sights after their sorts,
The white arms out in the breakers tirelessly
    tossing,
I, with bare feet, a child, the wind wafting my hair,
    Listened long and long.
Listened to keep, to sing, now translating the notes,
Following you, my brother.

    "Soothe! soothe! soothe!
Close on its wave soothes the wave behind,
And again another behind embracing and lapping,
    every one close,
But my love soothes not me, not me.

    "Low hangs the moon; it rose late,
It is lagging—O I think it is heavy with love, with
    love.

    "O madly the sea pushes upon the land,
With love, with love.

"O night! do I not see my love fluttering out
    among the breakers?
What is that little black thing I see there in the
    white?

"Loud! loud! loud!
Loud I call to you, my love!
High and clear I shoot my voice over the waves;
Surely you must know who is here, is here,
You must know who I am, my love.

"Low-hanging moon!
What is that dusky spot in your brown yellow?
O it is the shape, the shape of my mate!
O moon do not keep her from me any longer.

"Land! land! O land!
Whichever way I turn, O I think you could give me
 my mate back again, if you only would,
For I am almost sure I see her dimly whichever
 way I look.

"O rising stars!
Perhaps the one I want so much will rise, will rise
 with some of you.

"O throat! O trembling throat!
Sound clearer through the atmosphere!
Pierce the woods, the earth;
Somewhere listening to catch you must be the one
 I want.

"Shake out, carols!
Solitary here—the night's carols!
Carols of lonesome love! Death's carols!
Carols under that lagging, yellow, waning moon!

O under that moon where she droops almost down
    into the sea!
O reckless, despairing carols!

    "But soft! sink low;
Soft! let me just murmur;
And do you wait a moment, you husky-noised sea;
For somewhere I believe I heard my mate respond-
    ing to me,
So faint, I must be still, be still to listen;
But not altogether still, for then she might not
    come immediately to me.

    "Hither, my love!
Here I am! here!
With this just-sustained note I announced myself to
    you;
This gentle call is for you, my love, for you.

    "Do not be decoyed elsewhere!
That is the whistle of the wind—it is not my voice;
That is the fluttering, the fluttering of the spray;
Those are the shadows of leaves.

    "O darkness! O in vain!
O I am very sick and sorrowful.

    "O brown halo in the sky near the moon,
    drooping upon the sea!
O troubled reflection in the sea!
O throat! O throbbing heart!
And I singing uselessly, uselessly all the night.

"O past! O happy life! O songs of joy!
In the air, in the woods, over fields,
Loved! loved! loved! loved! loved!
But my mate no more, no more with me!
We two together no more."

The aria sinking,
All else continuing, the stars shining,
The winds blowing, the notes of the bird continuous echoing,
With angry moans the fierce old mother incessantly moaning,
On the sands of Paumanok's shore grey and rustling,
The yellow half-moon enlarged, sagging down, drooping, the face of the sea almost touching,
The boy ecstatic, with his bare feet the waves, with his hair the atmosphere dallying,
The love in the heart long pent, now loose, now at last tumultuously bursting,
The aria's meaning, the ears, the soul, swiftly depositing,
The strange tears down the cheeks coursing,
The colloquy there, the trio, each uttering,
The undertone, the savage old mother incessantly crying,
To the boy's soul's questions sullenly timing, some drown'd secret hissing,
To the outsetting bard.

WALT WHITMAN

SONG FROM "PIPPA PASSES"

The year's at the spring
And day's at the morn;
Morning's at seven;
The hillside's dew-pearled;
The lark's on the wing;
The snail's on the thorn:
God's in his heaven—
All's right with the world!

ROBERT BROWNING

SUMMER DAWN

Pray but one prayer for me 'twixt thy closed lips,
  Think but one thought of me up in the stars.
The summer night waneth, the morning light slips,
  Faint and grey 'twixt the leaves of the aspen, betwixt the cloud-bars,
That are patiently waiting there for the dawn:
  Patient and colourless, though Heaven's gold
Waits to float through them along with the sun.
Far out in the meadows, above the young corn,
  The heavy elms wait, and restless and cold
The uneasy wind rises; the roses are dun;

Through the long twilight they pray for the dawn,
Round the lone house in the midst of the corn.
  Speak but one word to me over the corn,
  Over the tender, bow'd locks of the corn.

WILLIAM MORRIS

TO THE HUMBLE-BEE

Burly, dozing humble-bee!
Where thou art is clime for me;
Let them sail for Porto Rique,
Far-off heats through seas to seek;
I will follow thee alone,
Thou animated torrid-zone!
Zigzag steerer, desert cheerer,
Let me chase thy waving lines;
Keep me nearer, me thy hearer,
Singing over shrubs and vines.

Insect lover of the sun,
Joy of thy dominion!
Sailor of the atmosphere,
Swimmer through the waves of air,
Voyager of light and noon,
Epicurean of June!
Wait, I prithee, till I come
Within earshot of thy hum,—
All without is martyrdom.

When the south wind, in May days,
With a net of shining haze
Silvers the horizon wall;
And, with softness touching all,
Tints the human countenance
With the colour of romance;
And infusing subtle heats,
Turns the sod to violets,—
Thou in sunny solitudes,
Rover of the underwoods,
The green silence dost displace
With thy mellow breezy bass.

Hot midsummer's petted crone,
Sweet to me thy drowsy tone
Tells of countless sunny hours,
Long days, and solid banks of flowers;
Of gulfs of sweetness without bound,
In Indian wildernesses found;
Of Syrian peace, immortal leisure,
Firmest cheer, and bird-like pleasure.

Aught unsavoury or unclean
Hath my insect never seen;
But violets, and bilberry bells,
Maple-sap, and daffodils,
Grass with green flag half-mast high,
Succory to match the sky,
Columbine with horn of honey,
Scented fern, and agrimony.

LONG DAYS, AND SOLID BANKS OF FLOWERS

Clover, catchfly, adder's-tongue,
And briar-roses, dwelt among:
All beside was unknown waste,
All was picture as he passed.

Wiser far than human seer,
Yellow-breeched philosopher,
Seeing only what is fair,
   Sipping only what is sweet,
Thou dost mock at fate and care,
   Leave the chaff and take the wheat.
When the fierce north-western blast
Cools sea and land so far and fast,—
Thou already slumberest deep;
Woe and want thou canst outsleep;
Want and woe, which torture us,
Thy sleep makes ridiculous.

RALPH WALDO EMERSON

THE BAREFOOT BOY

Blessings on thee, little man,
Barefoot boy, with cheek of tan!
With thy turned-up pantaloons,
And thy merry whistled tunes;
With thy red lip, redder still
Kissed by strawberries on the hill;
With the sunshine on thy face,
Through thy torn brim's jaunty grace;
From my heart I give thee joy,—
I was once a barefoot boy!
Prince thou art,—the grown-up man
Only is republican.
Let the million-dollared ride!
Barefoot, trudging at his side,
Thou hast more than he can buy
In the reach of ear and eye,—
Outward sunshine, inward joy:
Blessings on thee, barefoot boy!

Oh, for boyhood's painless play,
Sleep that wakes in laughing day,
Health that mocks the doctor's rules,
Knowledge never learned of schools,
Of the wild bee's morning chase,
Of the wild-flower's time and place,
Flight of fowl and habitude
Of the tenants of the wood;

How the tortoise bears his shell,
How the woodchuck digs his cell,
And the ground-mole sinks his well;
How the robin feeds her young,
How the oriole's nest is hung;
Where the whitest lilies blow,
Where the freshest berries grow,
Where the ground-nut trails its vine,
Where the wood-grape's clusters shine;
Of the black wasp's cunning way,
Mason of his walls of clay,
And the architectural plans
Of grey hornet artisans!
For, eschewing books and tasks,
Nature answers all he asks;
Hand in hand with her he walks,
Face to face with her he talks,
Part and parcel of her joy,—
Blessings on the barefoot boy!

Oh, for boyhood's time of June,
Crowding years in one brief moon,
When all things I heard or saw,
Me, their master, waited for.
I was rich in flowers and trees,
Humming-birds and honey-bees;
For my sport the squirrel played,
Plied the snouted mole his spade;
For my taste the blackberry cone

Purpled over hedge and stone;
Laughed the brook for my delight
Through the day and through the night,
Whispering at the garden wall,
Talked with me from fall to fall;
Mine the sand-rimmed pickerel pond,
Mine the walnut slopes beyond,
Mine, on bending orchard trees,
Apples of Hesperides!
Still as my horizon grew,
Larger grew my riches too;
All the world I saw or knew
Seemed a complex Chinese toy,
Fashioned for a barefoot boy!

Oh, for festal dainties spread,
Like my bowl of milk and bread;
Pewter spoon and bowl of wood,
On the door-stone, grey and rude!
O'er me, like a regal tent,
Cloudy-ribbed, the sunset bent,
Purple-curtained, fringed with gold,
Looped in many a wind-swung fold;
While for music came the play
Of the pied frog's orchestra;
And, to light the noisy choir,
Lit the fly his lamp of fire.
I was monarch: pomp and joy
Waited on the barefoot boy!

THE POETRY OF NATURE

      Cheerily, then, my little man,
Live and laugh, as boyhood can!
Though the flinty slopes be hard,
Stubble-speared the new-mown sward,
Every morn shall lead thee through
Fresh baptisms of the dew;
Every evening from thy feet
Shall the cool wind kiss the heat:
All too soon these feet must hide
In the prison cells of pride,
Lose the freedom of the sod,
Like a colt's for work be shod,
Made to tread the mills of toil,
Up and down in ceaseless moil;
Happy if their track be found
Never on forbidden ground;
Happy if they sink not in
Quick and treacherous sands of sin.
Ah! that thou couldst know thy joy,
Ere it passes, barefoot boy!
                    JOHN GREENLEAF WHITTIER

THE EVENING WIND

Spirit that breathest through my lattice, thou
  That cool'st the twilight of the sultry day!
Gratefully flows thy freshness round my brow;
  Thou hast been out upon the deep at play,
Riding all day the wild blue waves till now,
  Roughening their crests, and scattering high their
    spray,
And swelling the white sail. I welcome thee
To the scorched land, thou wanderer of the sea!

Nor I alone,—a thousand bosoms round
  Inhale thee in the fulness of delight;
And languid forms rise up, and pulses bound
  Livelier, at coming of the wind of night;
And languishing to hear thy grateful sound,
  Lies the vast inland, stretched beyond the
    sight.
Go forth into the gathering shade; go forth,—
God's blessing breathed upon the fainting earth!

Go, rock the little wood-bird in his nest;
  Curl the still waters, bright with stars; and
    rouse
The wide old wood from his majestic rest,
  Summoning, from the innumerable boughs,
The strange, deep harmonies that haunt his breast.
  Pleasant shall be thy way where meekly bows
The shutting flower, and darkling waters pass,
And where the o'ershadowing branches sweep the
    grass.

Stoop o'er the place of graves, and softly sway
  The sighing herbage by the gleaming stone,
That they who near the churchyard willows stray,
  And listen in the deepening gloom, alone,
May think of gentle souls who passed away,
  Like thy pure breath, into the vast unknown;
Sent forth from heaven along the sons of men,
And gone into the boundless heaven again.

The faint old man shall lean his silver head
  To feel thee; thou shalt kiss the child asleep,
And dry the moistened curls that overspread
  His temples, while his breathing grows more deep;
And they who stand about the sick man's bed
  Shall joy to listen to thy distant sweep,
And softly part his curtains to allow
Thy visit, grateful to his burning brow.

Go—but the circle of eternal change,
  Which is the life of nature, shall restore,
With sounds and sense from all thy mighty range,
Thee to thy birthplace of the deep once more;
Sweet odours in the sea-air, sweet and strange,
  Shall tell the homesick mariner of the shore;
And, listening to the murmur, he shall deem
He hears the rustling leaf and running stream.
WILLIAM CULLEN BRYANT

THE MIDGES DANCE ABOON THE BURN

  The midges dance aboon the burn;
    The dews begin to fa';
  The pairtricks down the rushy holm
    Set up their e'ening ca'.
  Now loud and clear the blackbird's sang
    Rings through the briary shaw,
    While, flitting gay, the swallows play
      Around the castle wa'.

Beneath the golden gloamin' sky
  The mavis mends her lay;
The redbreast pours his sweetest strains
  To charm the lingering day;
While weary yeldrins seem to wail
  Their little nestlings torn,
The merry wren, frae den to den,
  Gaes jinking through the thorn.

The roses fauld their silken leaves,
  The foxglove shuts its bell;
The honeysuckle and the birk
  Spread fragrance through the dell.
Let others crowd the giddy court
  Of mirth and revelry,
The simple joys that nature yields
  Are dearer far to me.

ROBERT TANNAHILL

BRIGHT STAR! WOULD I WERE STEADFAST AS THOU ART

Bright star! would I were steadfast as thou art—
Not in lone splendour hung aloft the night,
And watching, with eternal lids apart,
Like nature's patient, sleepless Eremite,
The moving waters at their priestlike task
Of pure ablution round earth's human shores,

Or gazing on the new soft fallen mask
Of snow upon the mountains and the moors—
No—yet still steadfast, still unchangeable,
Pillow'd upon my fair love's ripening breast,
To feel for ever its soft fall and swell,
Awake for ever in a sweet unrest,
  Still, still to hear her tender-taken breath,
  And so live ever—or else swoon to death.

JOHN KEATS

DAYBREAK

A WIND came up out of the sea,
And said, "O mists, make room for me!"

It hailed the ships, and cried, "Sail on,
Ye mariners, the night is gone."

And hurried landward far away,
Crying, "Awake! it is the day."

It said unto the forest, "Shout!
Hang all your leafy banners out!"

It touched the wood-bird's folded wing,
And said, "O bird, awake and sing."

And o'er the farms, "O chanticleer,
Your clarion blow; the day is near."

"A Wind came up out of the sea
And said O Mists make room for me."

It whispered to the fields of corn,
"Bow down, and hail the coming morn."

It shouted through the belfry-tower,
"Awake, O bell! proclaim the hour."

It crossed the churchyard with a sigh,
And said, "Not yet! in quiet lie."
HENRY WADSWORTH LONGFELLOW

THE MARSHES OF GLYNN
GLOOMS of the live-oaks, beautiful-braided and woven
With intricate shades of the vines that myriad-cloven
Clamber the forks of the multiform boughs,—
 Emerald twilights,—
 Virginal shy lights,
Wrought of the leaves to allure to the whisper of vows,
When lovers pace timidly down through the green
 colonnades
Of the dim sweet woods, of the dear dark woods,
 Of the heavenly woods and glades,
That run to the radiant marginal sand-beach within
 The wide sea-marshes of Glynn;—

Beautiful glooms, soft dusks in the noon-day fire,—
Wildwood privacies, closets of lone desire,

Chamber from chamber parted with wavering arras
  of leaves,—
Cells for the passionate pleasure of prayer to the
  soul that grieves,
Pure with a sense of the passing of saints through
  the wood,
Cool for the dutiful weighing of ill with good;—

O braided dusks of the oak and woven shades of the
  vine,
While the riotous noon-day sun of the June-day
  long did shine
Ye held me fast in your heart and I held you fast
  in mine;
But now when the noon is no more, and riot is rest,
And the sun is a-wait at the ponderous gate of the West,
And the slant yellow beam down with the wood-
  aisle doth seem.
Like a lane into heaven that leads from a dream,—
Ay, now, when my soul all day hath drunken soul
  of the oak,
And my heart is at ease from men, and the wearisome
  sound of the stroke
  Of the scythe of time and the trowel of trade is low,
  And belief overmasters doubt, and I know that I
    know,
  And my spirit is grown to a lordly great compass
    within,
That the length and the breadth and the sweep of
  the marshes of Glynn

Will work me no fear like the fear they have wrought me of yore
When length was fatigue, and when breadth was but bitterness sore,
And when terror and shrinking and dreary unnameable pain
Drew over me out of the merciless miles of the plain,—

Oh, now, afraid, I am fain to face
    The vast sweet visage of space.
To the edge of the wood I am drawn, I am drawn,
Where the grey beach glimmering runs, as a belt of the dawn,
    For a mete and a mark
    To the forest-dark:—
        So:
Affable live-oak, leaning low,—
Thus—with your favour—soft, with a reverent hand,
(Not lightly touching your person, Lord of the land!)
Bending your beauty aside, with a step I stand
On the firm-packed sand,
        Free
By a world of marsh that borders a world of sea.
    Sinuous southward and sinuous northward the shimmering band
    Of the sand-beach fastens the fringe of the marsh to the folds of the land.
    Inward and outward to northward and southward the beach-lines linger and curl

As a silver-wrought garment that clings to and
    follows the firm sweet limbs of a girl.
Vanishing, swerving, evermore curving again into
    sight,
Softly the sand-beach wavers away to a dim grey
    looping of light.
And what if behind me to westward the wall of the
    woods stands high?
The world lies east: how ample, the marsh and the
    sea and the sky!
A league and a league of marsh-grass, waist-high,
    broad in the blade,
Green, and all of a height, and unflecked with a
    light or a shade,
Stretch leisurely off, in a pleasant plain,
To the terminal blue of the main.
Oh, what is abroad in the marsh and the terminal sea?
  Somehow my soul seems suddenly free
From the weighing of fate and the sad discussion of sin,
By the length and the breadth and the sweep of the
    marshes of Glynn.

Ye marshes, how candid and simple and nothing-
    withholding and free
Ye publish yourselves to the sky and offer yourselves
    to the sea!
Tolerant plains, that suffer the sea and the rains
    and the sun,
Ye spread and span like the catholic man who hath
    mightily won

"Glooms of the live-oaks beautiful-braided and woven."

THE POETRY OF NATURE

God out of knowledge and good out of infinite pain,
And sight out of blindness and purity out of stain.

As the marsh-hen secretly builds on the watery sod,
Behold I will build me a nest on the greatness of God:
I will fly in the greatness of God as the marsh-hen flies
In the freedom that fills all the space 'twixt the
    marsh and the skies:
By so many roots as the marsh-grass sends in the sod
I will heartily lay me a-hold on the greatness of God:
Oh, like to the greatness of God is the greatness of
    within
The range of the marshes, the liberal marshes of
    Glynn.

And the sea lends large, as the marsh: lo, out of
    his plenty the sea
Pours fast: full soon the time of the flood-tide must
    be:
Look how the grace of the sea doth go
About- and about through the intricate channels
    that flow
    Here and there,
    Everywhere,
Till his waters have flooded the uttermost creeks
    and the low-lying lanes,
And the marsh is meshed with a million veins,
That like as with rosy and silvery essences flow
    In the rose-and-silver evening glow.

    Farewell, my lord Sun!
The creeks overflow: a thousand rivulets run
'Twixt the roots of the sod; the blades of the marsh-
        grass stir;
Passeth a hurrying sound of wings that westward
        whirr;
Passeth, and all is still; and the currents cease to run;
And the sea and the marsh are one.

How still the plains of the waters be!
The tide is in his ecstasy.
The tide is at his highest height;
    And it is night.

And now from the Vast of the Lord will the waters'
        sleep
Roll in on the souls of men,
But who will reveal to our waking ken
The forms that swim and the shapes that creep
        Under the waters of sleep?
And I would I could know what swimmeth below
        when the tide comes in
On the length and breadth of the marvellous
        marshes of Glynn.

                      SIDNEY LANIER

THE CHAMBERED NAUTILUS

This is the ship of pearl, which, poets feign,
    Sails the unshadowed main,—
    The venturous bark that flings
On the sweet summer wind its purpled wings
In gulfs enchanted, where the siren sings,
    And coral reefs lie bare,
Where the cold sea-maids rise to sun their streaming hair.

Its webs of living gauze no more unfurl;
    Wrecked is the ship of pearl!
    And every chambered cell,
Where its dim dreaming life was wont to dwell,
As the frail tenant shaped his growing shell,
    Before thee lies revealed,—
Its irised ceiling rent, its sunless crypt unsealed!

Year after year beheld the silent toil
    That spread his lustrous coil:
    Still, as the spiral grew,
He left the past year's dwelling for the new,
Stole with soft step its shining archway through,
    Built up its idle door,
Stretched in his last-found home, and knew the old no more.

Thanks for the heavenly message brought by thee,
    Child of the wandering sea,
    Cast from her lap, forlorn!
From thy dead lips a clearer note is born
Than ever Triton blew from wreathèd horn!
    While on mine ear it rings,
Through the deep caves of thought I hear a voice
    that sings:—

Build thee more stately mansions, O my soul,
    As the swift seasons roll!
    Leave thy low-vaulted past!
Let each new temple, nobler than the last,
Shut thee from heaven with a dome more vast,
    Till thou at length art free,
Leaving thine outgrown shell by life's unresting sea!

OLIVER WENDELL HOLMES

EACH AND ALL

LITTLE thinks, in the field, yon red-cloaked clown,
Of thee from the hill-top looking down;
The heifer that lows in the upland farm,
Far-heard, lows not thine ear to charm;
The sexton, tolling his bell at noon,
Deems not that great Napoleon
Stops his horse, and lists with delight,
Whilst his files sweep round yon Alpine height;

Nor knowest thou what argument
Thy life to thy neighbour's creed has lent.
All are needed by each one;
Nothing is fair or good alone.
I thought the sparrow's note from heaven,
Singing at dawn on the alder bough;
I brought him home, in his nest, at even;
He sings the song, but it cheers not now,
For I did not bring home the river and sky;—
He sang to my ear,—they sang to my eye.
The delicate shells lay on the shore;
The bubbles of the latest wave
Fresh pearls to their enamel gave,
And the bellowing of the savage sea
Greeted their safe escape to me.
I wiped away the weeds and foam,
I fetched my sea-born treasures home;
But the poor, unsightly, noisome things
Had left their beauty on the shore,
With the sun and the sand and the wild uproar
The lover watched his graceful maid,
As mid the virgin train she strayed,
Nor knew her beauty's best-attire
Was woven still by the snow-white choir.
At last she came to his hermitage,
Like the bird from the woodlands to the cage:-
The gay enchantment was undone,
A gentle wife, but fairy none.
Then I said, "I covet truth;

Beauty is unripe childhood's cheat;
I leave it behind with the games of youth":—
As I spoke, beneath my feet
The ground-pine curled its pretty wreath,
Running over the club-moss burrs;
I inhaled the violet's breath;
Around me stood the oaks and firs;
Pine-cones and acorns lay on the ground;
Over me soared the eternal sky,
Full of light and of deity;
Again I saw, again I heard,
The rolling river, the morning bird;—
Beauty through my senses stole;
I yielded myself to the perfect whole.

Ralph Waldo Emerson

IT IS A BEAUTEOUS EVENING, CALM AND FREE

It is a beauteous evening, calm and free,
    The holy time is quiet as a Nun
    Breathless with adoration; the broad sun
Is sinking down in its tranquillity;
The gentleness of heaven broods o'er the Sea:
    Listen! the mighty Being is awake,
    And doth with his eternal motion make
A sound like thunder—everlastingly.

Dear Child! dear Girl! that walkest with me here,
   If thou appear untouched by solemn thought,
   Thy nature is not therefore less divine:
Thou liest in Abraham's bosom all the year;
   And worshipp'st at the Temple's inner shrine,
   God being with thee when we know it not.
WILLIAM WORDSWORTH

THE WORLD IS TOO MUCH WITH US

THE world is too much with us; late and soon,
   Getting and spending, we lay waste our powers;
   Little we see in Nature that is ours;
We have given our hearts away, a sordid boon!
The Sea that bares her bosom to the moon;
   The winds that will be howling at all hours,
   And are up-gather'd now like sleeping flowers;
For this, for everything, we are out of tune;

It moves us not.—Great God! I'd rather be
   A Pagan suckled in a creed outworn;
So might I, standing on this pleasant lea,
   Have glimpses that would make me less forlorn;
Have sight of Proteus rising from the sea;
   Or hear old Triton blow his wreathèd horn.
WILLIAM WORDSWORTH

TINTERN ABBEY

FIVE years have past; five summers, with the length
Of five long winters! and again I hear
These waters, rolling from their mountain-springs
With a soft inland murmur.—Once again
Do I behold these steep and lofty cliffs,
That on a wild secluded scene impress
Thoughts of a more deep seclusion, and connect
The landscape with the quiet of the sky.
The day is come when I again repose
Here, under this dark sycamore, and view
These plots of cottage-ground, these orchard-tufts,
Which at this season, with their unripe fruits,
Are clad in one green hue, and lose themselves
'Mid groves and copses. Once again I see
These hedgerows, hardly hedgerows, little lines
Of sportive wood run wild: these pastoral farms,
Green to the very door; and wreaths of smoke
Sent up, in silence, from among the trees!
With some uncertain notice, as might seem
Of vagrant dwellers in the houseless woods,
Or of some Hermit's cave, where by his fire
The Hermit sits alone.
      These beauteous forms,
Through a long absence, have not been to me
As is a landscape to a blind man's eye:
But oft, in lonely rooms, and 'mid the din

Of towns and cities, I have owed to them,
In hours of weariness, sensations sweet,
Felt in the blood, and felt along the heart;
And passing even into my purer mind,
With tranquil restoration:—feelings too
Of unremembered pleasure: such, perhaps,
As have no slight or trivial influence
On that best portion of a good man's life,
His little, nameless, unremembered acts
Of kindness and of love. Nor less, I trust,
To them I may have owed another gift,
Of aspect more sublime; that blessed mood,
In which the burden of the mystery,
In which the heavy and the weary weight
Of all this unintelligible world,
Is lightened:—that serene and blessed mood
In which the affections gently lead us on,—
Until, the breath of this corporeal frame
And even the motion of our human blood
Almost suspended, we are laid asleep
In body, and become a living soul:
While with an eye made quiet by the power
Of harmony, and the deep power of joy,
We see into the life of things.
                                If this
Be but a vain belief, yet, oh! how oft—
In darkness and amid the many shapes
Of joyless daylight; when the fretful stir
Unprofitable, and the fever of the world,

Have hung upon the beatings of my heart—
How oft, in spirit, have I turned to thee,
O sylvan Wye! thou wanderer through the woods,
How often has my spirit turned to thee!
And now, with gleams of half-extinguished thought,
With many recognitions dim and faint,
And somewhat of a sad perplexity,
The picture of the mind revives again:
While here I stand, not only with the sense
Of present pleasure, but with pleasing thoughts
That in this moment there is life and food
For future years. And so I dare to hope,
Though changed, no doubt, from what I was when first
I came among these hills; when like a roe
I bounded o'er the mountains, by the sides
Of the deep rivers, and the lonely streams,
Wherever nature led: more like a man
Flying from something that he dreads, than one
Who sought the thing he loved. For Nature then
(The coarser pleasure of my boyish days,
And their glad animal movements all gone by)
To me was all in all.—I cannot paint
What then I was. The sounding cataract
Haunted me like a passion: the tall rock,
The mountain, and the deep and gloomy wood,
Their colours and their forms, were then to me
An appetite; a feeling and a love,
That had no need of a remoter charm,
By thoughts supplied, nor any interest

Unborrowed from the eye.—That time is past,
And all its aching joys are now no more,
And all its dizzy raptures. Not for this
Faint I, nor mourn nor murmur; other gifts
Have followed; for such loss, I would believe,
Abundant recompense. For I have learned
To look on Nature, not as in the hour
Of thoughtless youth; but hearing oftentimes
The still, sad music of humanity,
Nor harsh nor grating, though of ample power
To chasten and subdue. And I have felt
A presence that disturbs me with the joy
Of elevated thoughts; a sense sublime
Of something far more deeply interfused,
Whose dwelling is the light of setting suns,
And the round ocean, and the living air,
And the blue sky, and in the mind of man;
A motion and a spirit, that impels
All thinking things, all objects of all thought,
And rolls through all things. Therefore am I still
A lover of the meadows and the woods,
And mountains; and of all that we behold
From this green earth; of all the mighty world
Of eye, and ear,—both what they half create,
And what perceive; well pleased to recognise
In Nature and the language of the sense,
The anchor of my purest thoughts, the nurse,
The guide, the guardian of my heart, and soul
Of all my moral being.

THE POETRY OF NATURE

                Nor perchance,
If I were not thus taught, should I the more
Suffer my genial spirits to decay:
For thou art with me here upon the banks
Of this fair river; thou my dearest Friend,
My dear, dear Friend; and in thy voice I catch
The language of my former heart, and read
My former pleasures in the shooting lights
Of thy wild eyes. Oh! yet a little while
May I behold in thee what I was once,
My dear, dear Sister! and this prayer I make,
Knowing that Nature never did betray
The heart that loved her; 'tis her privilege,
Through all the years of this our life, to lead
From joy to joy: for she can so inform
The mind that is within us, so impress
With quietness and beauty, and so feed
With lofty thoughts, that neither evil tongues,
Rash judgments, nor the sneers of selfish men,
Nor greetings where no kindness is, nor all
The dreary intercourse of daily life,
Shall e'er prevail against us, or disturb
Our cheerful faith, that all which we behold
Is full of blessings. Therefore let the moon
Shine on thee in thy solitary walk;
And let the misty mountain-winds be free
To blow against thee: and, in after years,
When these wild ecstasies shall be matured
Into a sober pleasure; when thy mind

Shall be a mansion for all lovely forms,
Thy memory be as a dwelling-place
For all sweet sounds and harmonies; oh! then,
If solitude, or fear, or pain, or grief,
Should be thy portion, with what healing thoughts
Of tender joy wilt thou remember me,
And these my exhortations! Nor, perchance,—
If I should be where I no more can hear
Thy voice, nor catch from thy wild eyes these gleams
Of past existence—wilt thou then forget
That on the banks of this delightful stream
We stood together; and that I, so long
A worshipper of Nature, hither came
Unwearied in that service: rather say
With warmer love—oh! with far deeper zeal
Of holier love. Nor wilt thou then forget
That after many wanderings, many years
Of absence, these steep woods and lofty cliffs,
And this green pastoral landscape, were to me
More dear, both for themselves and for thy sake!
WILLIAM WORDSWORTH

ODE TO EVENING

If aught of oaten stop, or pastoral song,
May hope, chaste eve, to soothe thy modest ear,
    Like thy own solemn springs,
    Thy springs, and dying gales,

O nymph reserved, while now the bright-hair'd sun
Sits in yon western tent, whose cloudy skirts,
    With brede ethereal wove,
    O'erhang his wavy bed:

Now air is hush'd, save where the weak-eyed bat
With short, shrill shriek, flits by on leathern wing;
    Or where the beetle winds
    His small but sullen horn,

As oft he rises 'midst the twilight path,
Against the pilgrim borne in heedless hum:
    Now teach me, maid composed,
    To breathe some soften'd strain,

Whose numbers, stealing through thy darkening vale,
May, not unseemly, with its stillness suit,
    As, musing slow, I hail
    Thy genial loved return!

For when thy folding-star arising shows
His paly circlet, at his warning lamp
    The fragrant hours, and elves
    Who slept in flowers the day,

And many a nymph who wreathes her brows with sedge,
And sheds the freshening dew, and, lovelier still,
    The pensive pleasures sweet
    Prepare thy shadowy car.

Then lead, calm votaress, where some sheety lake
Cheers the lone heath, or some time-hallow'd pile,
    Or upland fallows grey
    Reflect its last cool gleam

But when chill blustering winds, or driving rain,
Forbid my willing feet, be mine the hut,
    That from the mountain's side,
    Views wilds, and swelling floods,

And hamlets brown, and dim-discover'd spires;
And hears their simple bell, and marks o'er all
    Thy dewy fingers draw
    The gradual dusky veil.

While spring shall pour his showers, as oft he wont,
And bathe thy breathing tresses, meekest eve!
    While summer loves to sport
    Beneath thy lingering light;

While sallow autumn fills thy lap with leaves;
Or winter, yelling through the troublous air,
    Affrights thy shrinking train,
    And rudely rends thy robes;

So long, sure-found beneath the sylvan shed,
Shall fancy, friendship, science, rose-lipp'd health,
    Thy gentlest influence own,
    And hymn thy favourite name!

                        WILLIAM COLLINS

TEARS, IDLE TEARS

Tears, idle tears, I know not what they mean,
Tears from the depth of some divine despair
Rise in the heart, and gather to the eyes,
In looking on the happy Autumn-fields,
And thinking of the days that are no more.

Fresh as the first beam glittering on a sail,
That brings our friends up from the underworld,
Sad as the last which reddens over one
That sinks with all we love below the verge;
So sad, so fresh, the days that are no more.

Ah, sad and strange as in dark summer dawns
The earliest pipe of half-awaken'd birds
To dying ears, when unto dying eyes
The casement slowly grows a glimmering square;
So sad, so strange, the days that are no more.

Dear as remember'd kisses after death,
And sweet as those by hopeless fancy feign'd
On lips that are for others; deep as love,
Deep as first love, and wild with all regret;
O Death in Life, the days that are no more!

LORD TENNYSON

THE LIGHT OF STARS

The night is come, but not too soon;
    And sinking silently,
All silently, the little moon
    Drops down behind the sky.

There is no light in earth or heaven
    But the cold light of stars;
And the first watch of night is given
    To the red planet Mars.

Is it the tender star of love?
    The star of love and dreams?
Oh no! from that blue tent above
    A hero's armour gleams.

And earnest thoughts within me rise,
    When I behold afar,
Suspended in the evening skies,
    The shield of that red star.

O star of strength! I see thee stand
    And smile upon my pain;
Thou beckonest with thy mailèd hand,
    And I am strong again.

"Ah, sad and strange as in dark summer dawns."

Within my breast there is no light
  But the cold light of stars;
I give the first watch of the night
  To the red planet Mars.

The star of the unconquered will,
  He rises in my breast,
Serene, and resolute, and still,
  And calm, and self-possessed.

And thou, too, whosoe'er thou art,
  That readest this brief psalm,
As one by one thy hopes depart,
  Be resolute and calm.

Oh, fear not in a world like this,
  And thou shalt know ere long,
Know how sublime a thing it is
  To suffer and be strong.

HENRY WADSWORTH LONGFELLOW

TO AUTUMN

SEASON of mists and mellow fruitfulness,
  Close bosom-friend of the maturing sun;
Conspiring with him how to load and bless
  With fruit the vines that round the thatch-eves run;
To bend with apples the moss'd cottage-trees,
  And fill all fruit with ripeness to the core;

To swell the gourd, and plump the hazel shells
With a sweet kernel; to set budding more,
　And still more, later flowers for the bees,
　Until they think warm days will never cease,
　　For Summer has o'er-brimm'd their clammy cells.

Who hath not seen thee oft amid thy store?
　Sometimes whoever seeks abroad may find
Thee sitting careless on a granary floor,
　Thy hair soft-lifted by the winnowing wind;
Or on a half-reap'd furrow sound asleep,
　Drows'd with the fume of poppies, while thy hook
　　Spares the next swath and all its twinèd flowers:
And sometimes like a gleaner thou dost keep
　Steady thy laden head across a brook;
　Or by a cider-press, with patient look,
　　Thou watchest the last oozings, hours by hours.

Where are the songs of Spring? Ay, where are they?
　Think not of them, thou hast thy music too,—
While barrèd clouds bloom the soft-dying day,
　And touch the stubble-plains with rosy hue;
Then in a wailful choir the small gnats mourn
　Among the river sallows, borne aloft
　　Or sinking as the light wind lives or dies;
And full-grown lambs loud bleat from hilly bourn;
　Hedge-crickets sing; and now with treble soft
　The redbreast whistles from a garden-croft,
　　And gathering swallows twitter in the skies.

　　　　　　　　　　　　　　　JOHN KEATS

SONG

A SPIRIT haunts the year's last hours
Dwelling amid these yellowing bowers:
    To himself he talks;
For at eventide, listening earnestly,
At his work you may hear him sob and sigh
    In the walks;
    Earthward he boweth the heavy stalks
Of the mouldering flowers:
  Heavily hangs the broad sunflower
    Over its grave i' the earth so chilly;
  Heavily hangs the hollyhock,
    Heavily hangs the tiger-lily.

The air is damp, and hush'd, and close,
As a sick man's room when he taketh repose
   An hour before death;
My very heart faints and my whole soul grieves
At the moist rich smell of the rotting leaves,
   And the breath
     Of the fading edges of box beneath,
And the year's last rose.
   Heavily hangs the broad sunflower
     Over its grave i' the earth so chilly;
   Heavily hangs the hollyhock,
     Heavily hangs the tiger-lily.

LORD TENNYSON

TO A MOUSE

WEE, sleekit, cowrin', tim'rous beastie;
Oh, what a panic's in thy breastie!
Thou need not start awa sae hasty
   Wi' bickering brattle!
I wad be laith to rin an' chase thee
   Wi' murdering pattle!

I'm truly sorry man's dominion
Has broken nature's social union,
An' justifies that ill opinion,
   Which makes thee startle
At me, thy poor, earth-born companion
   An' fellow mortal!

I doubt na, whiles, but thou may thieve;
What then? poor beastie, thou maun live!
A daimen icker in a thrave
    'S a sma' request;
I'll get a blessin' wi' the lave,
      An' never miss't!

Thy wee-bit housie, too, in ruin!
Its silly wa's the win's are strewin'!
And naething, now, to big a new ane
    O' foggage green!
An' bleak December's win's ensuin',
      Baith snell an' keen!

Thou saw the fields laid bare and waste
An' weary winter comin' fast,
An' cozie here, beneath the blast,
    Thou thought to dwell,
Till crash! the cruel coulter past
      Out thro' thy cell.

That wee bit heap o' leaves an' stibble,
Has cost thee mony a weary nibble!
Now thou's turn'd out, for a' thy trouble
    But house or hald,
To thole the winter's sleety dribble,
      An' cranreuch cauld!

But Mousie, thou art no thy lane,
In proving foresight may be vain:

The best-laid schemes o' mice an' men,
    Gang aft agley,
An' lea'e us nought but grief an' pain,
    For promis'd joy.

Still thou art blest, compared wi' me!
The present only toucheth thee:
But och! I backward cast my e'e,
    On prospects drear!
An' forward, tho' I canna see,
    I guess an' fear.

ROBERT BURNS

TO THE FRINGED GENTIAN

Thou blossom bright with autumn dew,
And coloured with the heavens' own blue,
That openest when the quiet light
Succeeds the keen and frosty night.

Thou comest not when violets lean
O'er wandering brooks and springs unseen,
Or columbines, in purple dressed,
Nod o'er the ground-bird's hidden nest.

Thou waitest late and com'st alone,
When woods are bare and birds are flown,
And frosts and shortening days portend
The aged Year is near his end.

Then doth thy sweet and quiet eye
Look through its fringes to the sky,
Blue—blue—as if that sky let fall
A flower from its cerulean wall.

I would that thus, when I shall see
The hour of death draw near to me,
Hope, blossoming within my heart,
May look to heaven as I depart.
                          WILLIAM CULLEN BRYANT

SEAWEED

WHEN descends on the Atlantic
    The gigantic
Storm-wind of the equinox,
Landward in his wrath he scourges
    The toiling surges,
Laden with seaweed from the rocks:

From Bermuda's reefs; from the edges
    Of sunken ledges,
In some far-off, bright Azore;
From Bahama, and the dashing,
    Silver flashing
Surges of San Salvador;

"Laden with seaweed from the rocks."

From the tumbling surf, that buries
    The Orkneyan skerries,
Answering the hoarse Hebrides;
And from wrecks of ships, and drifting
    Spars, uplifting
On the desolate rainy seas;—

Ever drifting, drifting, drifting
    On the shifting
Currents of the restless main;
Till in sheltered coves, and reaches
    Of sandy beaches,
All have found repose again.

So when storms of wild emotion
    Strike the ocean
Of the poet's soul, erelong
From each cave and rocky fastness,
    In its vastness,
Floats some fragment of a song:

From the far-off isles enchanted,
    Heaven has planted
With the golden fruit of Truth;
From the flashing surf, whose vision
    Gleams Elysian
In the tropic clime of Youth;

THE POETRY OF NATURE

    From the strong Will, and the Endeavour
        That for ever
    Wrestle with the tides of Fate;
    From the wreck of Hopes far-scattered,
        Tempest-shattered,
    Floating waste and desolate;—

    Ever drifting, drifting, drifting
        On the shifting
    Currents of the restless heart;
    Till at length in books recorded,
        They, like hoarded
    Household words, no more depart.
            HENRY WADSWORTH LONGFELLOW

AUTUMN

I saw old Autumn in the misty morn
Stand shadowless like Silence, listening
To silence, for no lonely bird would sing
Into his hollow ear from woods forlorn,
Nor lowly hedge nor solitary thorn;
Shaking his languid locks all dewy bright
With tangled gossamer that fell by night,
    Pearling his coronet of golden corn.

Where are the songs of summer?—With the sun,
Oping the dusky eyelids of the south,
Till shade and silence waken up as one,
And Morning sings with a warm odorous mouth.

"I saw old Autumn in the misty morn."

Where are the merry birds?—Away, away,
On panting wings through the inclement skies,
  Lest owls should prey
  Undazzled at noon-day,
And tear with horny beak their lustrous eyes.

Where are the blooms of summer?—In the west,
Blushing their last to the last sunny hours,
When the mild Eve by sudden Night is prest
Like tearful Proserpine, snatch'd from her flow'rs
  To a gloomy breast.
Where is the pride of summer,—the green prime,-
The many, many leaves all twinkling?—Three
On the moss'd elm; three on the naked lime
Trembling,—and one upon the old oak tree!
  Where is the Dryad's immortality?—
Gone into mournful cypress and dark yew,
Or wearing the long gloomy Winter through
  In the smooth holly's green eternity.

The squirrel gloats o'er his accomplish'd hoard,
The ants have brimm'd their garners with ripe
    grain,
  And honey bees have stored
The sweets of summer in their luscious cells;
The swallows all have wing'd across the main;
But here the Autumn melancholy dwells.
  And sighs her tearful spells
Amongst the sunless shadows of the plain.

Alone, alone,
  Upon a mossy stone,
She sits and reckons up the dead and gone,
With the last leaves of a love-rosary;
Whilst all the wither'd world looks drearily,
Like a dim picture of the drowned past
In the hush'd mind's mysterious far-away,
Doubtful what ghostly thing will steal the last
Into that distance, grey upon the grey.

O go and sit with her, and be o'ershaded
Under the languid downfall of her hair;
She wears a coronal of flowers faded
Upon her forehead, and a face of care;—
There is enough of wither'd everywhere
To make her bower,—and enough of gloom;
There is enough of sadness to invite,
If only for the rose that died, whose doom
Is Beauty's—she that with the living bloom
Of conscious cheeks most beautifies the light;
There is enough of sorrowing, and quite
Enough of bitter fruits the earth doth bear,—
Enough of chilly droppings for her bowl;
Enough of fear, and shadowy despair,
To frame her cloudy prison for the soul!

THOMAS HOOD

THE DEATH OF THE FLOWERS

The melancholy days are come, the saddest of the year,
Of wailing winds, and naked woods, and meadows brown and sear.
Heaped in the hollows of the grove, the autumn leaves lie dead;
They rustle to the eddying gust, and to the rabbit's tread;
The robin and the wren are flown, and from the shrubs the jay,
And from the wood-top calls the crow through all the gloomy day.

Where are the flowers, the fair young flowers, that lately sprang and stood
In brighter light and softer airs, a beauteous sisterhood?
Alas! they are all in their graves, the gentle race of flowers
Are ying in their lowly beds, with the fair and good of ours.
The rain is falling where they lie, but the cold November rain
Calls not from out the gloomy earth the lovely ones again.

The wind-flower and the violet, they perished long ago,
And the briar-rose and the orchids died amid the summer glow;

**HEAPED IN THE HOLLOWS OF THE GROVE,
THE AUTUMN LEAVES LIE DEAD.**

But on the hills the golden rod, and the aster in the wood,
And the yellow sunflower by the brook in autumn beauty stood,
Till fell the frost from the clear cold heaven, as falls the plague on men,
And the brightness of their smile was gone, from upland, glade, and glen.

And now, when comes the calm mild day, as still such days will come,
To call the squirrel and the bee from out their winter home;
When the sound of dropping nuts is heard, though all trees are still,
And twinkle in the smoky light the waters of the rill,
The south-wind searches for the flowers whose fragrance late he bore,
And sighs to find them in the wood and by the stream no more.

And then I think of one who in her youthful beauty died,
The fair meek blossom that grew up and faded by my side.
In the cold moist earth we laid her, when the forests cast the leaf,
And we wept that one so lovely should have a life so brief:

Yet not unmeet it was that one, like that young
    friend of ours,
So gentle and so beautiful, should perish with the
    flowers.
WILLIAM CULLEN BRYANT

ODE TO THE WEST WIND

O WILD West Wind, thou breath of Autumn's being,
  Thou, from whose unseen presence the leaves dead
Are driven, like ghosts from an enchanter fleeing.

  Yellow, and black, and pale, and hectic red,
Pestilence-stricken multitudes: O thou,
  Who chariotest to their dark wintry bed

The wingèd seeds, where they lie cold and low,
  Each like a corpse within its grave, until
Thine azure sister of the spring shall blow

  Her clarion o'er the dreaming earth, and fill
(Driving sweet buds like flocks to feed in air)
  With living hues and odours plain and hill:

Wild Spirit, which art moving everywhere;
Destroyer and preserver; hear, oh, hear!

THE POETRY OF NATURE

Thou on whose stream, 'mid the steep sky's commotion,
   Loose clouds like earth's decaying leaves are shed,
Shook from the tangled boughs of Heaven and Ocean,

   Angels of rain and lightning: they are spread
On the blue surface of thine airy surge,
   Like the bright hair uplifted from the head

Of some fierce Mænad, even from the dim verge
   Of the horizon to the zenith's height,
The locks of the approaching storm. Thou dirge

   Of the dying year, to which this closing night
Will be the dome of a vast sepulchre,
   Vaulted with all thy congregated might

Of vapours, from whose solid atmosphere
Black rain, and fire, and hail will burst: Oh, hear!

Thou who didst waken from his summer dreams
   The blue Mediterranean, where he lay,
Lull'd by the coil of his crystalline streams,

   Beside a pumice isle in Baiæ's bay,
And saw in sleep old palaces and towers
   Quivering within the wave's intenser day,

THE POETRY OF NATURE

All overgrown with azure moss and flowers
  So sweet, the sense faints picturing them! Thou
For whose path the Atlantic's level powers

  Cleave themselves into chasms, while far below
The sea-blooms and the oozy woods which wear
  The sapless foliage of the ocean, know

Thy voice, and suddenly grow grey with fear,
And tremble and despoil themselves: Oh, hear!

If I were a dead leaf thou mightest bear;
  If I were a swift cloud to fly with thee;
A wave to pant beneath thy power, and share

  The impulse of thy strength, only less free
Than thou, O incontrollable! if even
  I were as in my boyhood, and could be

The comrade of thy wanderings over heaven,
  As then, when to outstrip thy skiey speed
Scarce seem'd a vision; I would ne'er have striven

  As thus with thee in prayer in my sore need.
Oh, lift me as a wave, a leaf, a cloud!
  I fall upon the thorns of life! I bleed!

A heavy weight of hours has chain'd and bow'd
One too like thee: tameless, and swift, and proud.

Make me thy lyre, even as the forest is:
  What if my leaves are falling like its own!
The tumult of thy mighty harmonies

  Will take from both a deep, autumnal tone,
Sweet thou in sadness. Be thou, Spirit fierce,
  My spirit! Be thou me, impetuous one!

Drive my dead thoughts over the universe
  Like wither'd leaves, to quicken a new birth!
And, by the incantation of this verse,

  Scatter, as from an unextinguished hearth
Ashes and sparks, my words among mankind!
  Be through my lips to unawaken'd earth

The trumpet of a prophecy! O wind,
If Winter comes, can Spring be far behind?
PERCY BYSSHE SHELLEY

NATURE

As a fond mother, when the day is o'er,
  Leads by the hand her little child to bed,
  Half willing, half reluctant to be led,
And leave his broken playthings on the floor,
Still gazing at them through the open door,

Nor wholly reassured and comforted
  By promises of others in their stead,
Which, though more splendid, may not please him
    more;
So Nature deals with us, and takes away
  Our playthings one by one, and by the hand
    Leads us to rest so gently, that we go
Scarce knowing if we wish to go or stay,
  Being too full of sleep to understand
    How far the unknown transcends the what we
      know.
                    HENRY WADSWORTH LONGFELLOW

THE FIRST SNOWFALL

THE snow had begun in the gloaming,
  And busily all the night
Had been heaping field and highway
  With a silence deep and white.

Every pine and fir and hemlock
  Wore ermine too dear for an earl,
And the poorest twig on the elm-tree
  Was ridged inch-deep with pearl.

From sheds new-roofed with Carrara
  Came Chanticleer's muffled crow,
The stiff rails softened to swan's-down,
  And still fluttered down the snow.

I stood and watched by the window
    The noiseless work of the sky,
And the sudden flurries of snow-birds,
    Like brown leaves whirling by.

I thought of a mound in sweet Auburn
    Where a little headstone stood;
How the flakes were folding it gently,
    As did robins the babes in the wood.

Up spoke our own little Mabel,
    Saying, "Father, who makes it snow?"
And I told of the good All-father
    Who cares for us here below.

Again I looked at the snowfall,
    And thought of the leaden sky
That arched o'er our first great sorrow,
    When that mound was heaped so high.

I remembered the gradual patience
    That fell from that cloud like snow,
Flake by flake, healing and hiding
    The scar that renewed our woe.

And again to the child I whispered,
    "The snow that husheth all,
Darling, the merciful Father
    Alone can make it fall!"

**HEAPING FIELD AND HIGHWAY
WITH A SILENCE DEEP AND WHITE**

> Then, with eyes that saw not, I kissed her;
> And she, kissing back, could not know
> That *my* kiss was given to her sister,
> Folded close under deepening snow.

JAMES RUSSELL LOWELL

INFLUENCE OF NATURAL OBJECTS
IN CALLING FORTH AND STRENGTHENING THE IMAGINATION IN BOYHOOD AND EARLY YOUTH

WISDOM and Spirit of the universe!
Thou Soul, that art the Eternity of thought!
And giv'st to forms and images a breath
And everlasting motion! not in vain,
By day or star-light, thus from my first dawn
Of childhood didst thou intertwine for me
The passions that build up our human soul;
Not with the mean and vulgar works of Man;
But with high objects, with enduring things,
With life and nature; purifying thus
The elements of feeling and of thought,
And sanctifying by such discipline
Both pain and fear,—until we recognise
A grandeur in the beatings of the heart.
 Nor was this fellowship vouchsafed to me
With stinted kindness. In November days,
When vapours rolling down the valleys made

A lonely scene more lonesome; among woods
At noon; and 'mid the calm of summer nights,
When, by the margin of the trembling lake,
Beneath the gloomy hills, homeward I went
In solitude, such intercourse was mine:
Mine was it in the fields both day and night,
And by the waters, all the summer long.
And in the frosty season, when the sun
Was set, and, visible for many a mile,
The cottage-windows through the twilight blazed,
I heeded not the summons: happy time
It was indeed for all of us; for me
It was a time of rapture! Clear and loud
The village-clock tolled six—I wheeled about,
Proud and exulting like an untired horse
That cares not for his home.—All shod with steel
We hissed along the polished ice, in games
Confederate, imitative of the chase
And woodland pleasures,—the resounding horn,
The pack loud-chiming, and the hunted hare.
So through the darkness and the cold we flew,
And not a voice was idle: with the din
Smitten, the precipices rang aloud;
The leafless trees and every icy crag
Tinkled like iron; while far distant hills
Into the tumult sent an alien sound
Of melancholy, not unnoticed, while the stars,
Eastward, were sparkling clear, and in the west
The orange sky of evening died away.

    Not seldom from the uproar I retired
Into a silent bay, or sportively
Glanced sideway, leaving the tumultuous throng,
To cut across the reflex of a star;
Image, that, flying still before me, gleamed
Upon the glassy plain: and oftentimes,
When we had given our bodies to the wind,
And all the shadowy banks on either side
Came sweeping through the darkness, spinning still
The rapid line of motion, then at once
Have I, reclining back upon my heels,
Stopped short; yet still the solitary cliffs
Wheeled by me—even as if the earth had rolled
With visible motion her diurnal round!
Behind me did they stretch in solemn train,
Feebler and feebler, and I stood and watched
Till all was tranquil as a summer sea.
WILLIAM WORDSWORTH

THE SNOWSTORM

ANNOUNCED by all the trumpets of the sky,
Arrives the snow, and, driving o'er the fields,
Seems nowhere to alight: the whited air
Hides hills and woods, the river, and the heaven,
And veils the farmhouse at the garden's end.
The sled and traveller stopped, the courier's feet
Delayed, all friends shut out, the housemates sit

Around the radiant fireplace, enclosed
In a tumultuous privacy of storm.
  Come, see the north wind's masonry.
Out of an unseen quarry evermore
Furnished with tile, the fierce artificer
Curves his white bastions with projected roof
Round every windward stake, or tree, or door.
Speeding, the myriad-handed, his wild work
So fanciful, so savage, naught cares he
For number or proportion. Mockingly,
On coop or kennel he hangs Parian wreaths;
A swan-like form invests the hidden thorn;
Fills up the farmer's lane from wall to wall,
Maugre the farmer's sighs; and at the gate
A tapering turret overtops the work.
And when his hours are numbered, and the world
Is all his own, retiring, as he were not,
Leaves, when the sun appears, astonished Art
To mimic in slow structures, stone by stone,
Built in an age, the mad wind's night-work,
The frolic architecture of the snow.

RALPH WALDO EMERSON

SONNET

THAT time of year thou mayest in me behold
When yellow leaves, or none, or few, do hang
Upon those boughs which shake against the cold—
Bare ruin'd choirs, where late the sweet birds sang

In me thou see'st the twilight of such day
As after sunset fadeth in the west;
Which by and by black night doth take away,
Death's second self, that seals up all in rest.
In me thou see'st the glowing of such fire,
That on the ashes of his youth doth lie,
As the death-bed whereon it must expire,
Consumed with that which it was nourish'd by.
  This thou perceivest, which makes thy love more
     strong,
  To love that well which thou must leave ere long.
WILLIAM SHAKESPEARE

BLOW, BLOW, THOU WINTER WIND
(FROM "AS YOU LIKE IT")

Blow, blow, thou winter wind,
  Thou art not so unkind
    As man's ingratitude;
  Thy tooth is not so keen,
  Because thou art not seen,
    Although thy breath be rude.
Heigh-ho! sing heigh-ho! unto the green holly:
Most friendship is feigning, most loving mere folly:
  Then, heigh-ho, the holly!
    This life is most jolly.

  Freeze, freeze, thou bitter sky,
  Thou dost not bite so nigh

        As benefits forgot:
Though thou the waters warp,
Thy sting is not so sharp
        As friend remember'd not.
Heigh-ho! sing, heigh-ho! unto the green holly:
Most friendship is feigning, most loving mere folly:
        Then, heigh-ho, the holly!
        This life is most jolly.

WILLIAM SHAKESPEARE

ON THE GRASSHOPPER AND CRICKET

THE poetry of earth is never dead:
    When all the birds are faint with the hot sun,
    And hide in cooling trees, a voice will run
From hedge to hedge about the new-mown mead;
That is the Grasshopper's—he takes the lead
    In summer luxury,—he has never done
    With his delights; for when tired out with fun,
He rests at ease beneath some pleasant weed.
    The poetry of earth is ceasing never:
    On a lone winter evening, when the frost
Has wrought a silence, from the stove there shrills
The Cricket's song, in warmth increasing ever,
    And seems to one, in drowsiness half lost,
The Grasshopper's among some grassy hills.

JOHN KEATS

"Blow, Blow, thou Winter Wind."

THE DEATH OF THE OLD YEAR

FULL knee-deep lies the winter-snow,
   And the winter winds are wearily sighing:
Toll ye the church-bell sad and slow
And tread softly and speak low,
For the old year lies a-dying.
        Old year, you must not die;
        You came to us so readily,
        You lived with us so steadily,
        Old year, you shall not die.

He lieth still: he doth not move:
He will not see the dawn of day.
He hath no other life above.
He gave me a friend, and a true true-love,
And the New-year will take 'em away.
      Old year, you must not go;
      So long as you have been with us,
      Such joy as you have seen with us,
      Old year, you shall not go.

He froth'd his bumpers to the brim;
A jollier year we shall not see.
But tho' his eyes are waxing dim,
And tho' his foes speak ill of him,
He was a friend to me.
      Old year, you shall not die;
      We did so laugh and cry with you,
      I've half a mind to die with you,
      Old year, if you must die.

He was full of joke and jest,
But all his merry quips are o'er.
To see him die, across the waste
His son and heir doth ride post-haste,
But he'll be dead before.
      Every one for his own,
      The night is starry and cold, my friend,
      And the New-year blithe and bold, my friend,
      Comes up to take his own.

THE POETRY OF NATURE

How hard he breathes! over the snow
I heard just now the crowing cock.
The shadows flicker to and fro:
The cricket chirps: the light burns low:
'Tis nearly twelve o'clock.
      Shake hands, before you die.
      Old year, we'll dearly rue for you:
      What is it we can do for you?
      Speak out before you die.

His face is growing sharp and thin.
Alack! our friend is gone.
Close up his eyes: tie up his chin:
Step from the corpse, and let him in
That standeth there alone,
      And waiteth at the door.
      There's a new foot on the floor, my friend,
      And a new face at the door, my friend,
      A new face at the door.

                            LORD TENNYSON